FADE OUT — FADE IN

FADE OUT– FADE IN

BOOK AND LYRICS BY

*Betty
Comden* & *Adolph
Green*

MUSIC BY

Jule Styne

RANDOM HOUSE · NEW YORK

FADE OUT—FADE IN *was first presented by Lester Osterman and Jule Styne at the Mark Hellinger Theatre, New York City, on May 26, 1964, with the following cast:*

(In order of appearance)

AUTOGRAPH KIDS	Roger Allan Raby, Charlene Mehl
HELGA SIXTREES	Judy Cassmore
POPS	Frank Tweddell
BILLY VESPERS	Glenn Kezer
ROSCOE	Bob Neukum
BYRON PRONG	Jack Cassidy
LYMAN	John Dorrin
REX	Darrell J. Askey
HOPE SPRINGFIELD	Carol Burnett
CHAUFFEUR	William Louther
GIRL	Wendy Taylor
FIRST COWBOY EXTRA	Stephen Elmore
SECOND COWBOY EXTRA	Fred Cline
GANGSTER EXTRA	Gene Varrone
RALPH GOVERNOR	Mitchell Jason
RUDOLF GOVERNOR	Dick Patterson
GEORGE GOVERNOR	Howard Kahl
FRANK GOVERNOR	John Dorrin
HAROLD GOVERNOR	Gene Varrone
ARNOLD GOVERNOR	Stephen Elmore
CONVICTS	Gene Kelton, William Louther, Ed Pfeiffer, James Von Weiss
MYRA MAY MELROSE	Virginia Payne
SEAMSTRESS	Diane Arnold
CUSTER CORKLEY	Dan Resin
MAX WELCH	Richard Frisch
LOU WILLIAMS	Tiger Haynes

1939000

DORA DAILEY	Aileen Poe
DR. ANTON TRAURIG	Reuben Singer
LIONEL Z. GOVERNOR	Lou Jacobi
GLORIA CURRIE	Tina Louise
MADAME BARRYMORE	Penny Egelston

SINGING ENSEMBLE: Sean Allan, Jackie Alloway, Darrell J. Askey, Fred Cline, John Dorrin, Trish Dwelley, Stephen Elmore, Richard Frisch, Howard Kahl, Carolyn Kemp, Betty Kent, Glenn Kezer, Mari Nettum, Bob Neukum, Roger Allan Raby, Jo Tract, Gene Varrone.

DANCING ENSEMBLE: Virginia Allen, Diane Arnold, Judy Cassmore, Diana Ede, Ernie Horvath, Gene Kelton, William Louther, Charlene Mehl, Judy Newman, Jodi Perselle, Ed Pfeiffer, Carolsue Shaer, Patricia Sigris, Roy Smith, Bill Stanton, Wendy Taylor, James Von Weiss. (Lead Dancer: Don Crichton)

Directed by George Abbott

Dances and musical numbers staged by Ernest Flatt
Settings and lighting by William and Jean Eckart
Costumes by Donald Brooks   *Hair styles by* Ernest Adler
Musical direction by Colin Romoff
Orchestrations by Ralph Burns and Ray Ellis
Vocal arrangements by Buster Davis
Dance music arranged by Richard De Benedictis

SYNOPSIS OF SCENES

The action takes place in Hollywood and Vienna in the mid-1930's.

Act One

Act Two

MUSICAL NUMBERS

Act One

"It's Good to Be Back Home" HOPE

"Fear" RUDOLF, RALPH and OTHER NEPHEWS

Reprise: "Fear" BYRON and NEPHEWS

"Call Me Savage" HOPE and RUDOLF

"The Usher from the Mezzanine" HOPE

"My Heart Is Like a Violin" BYRON

"I'm With You" HOPE, BYRON and ENSEMBLE

"Notice Me" RUDOLF

"My Fortune Is My Face" BYRON

"A Girl to Remember" HOPE

Act Two

"Close Harmony" L.Z., BYRON, GLORIA and OTHERS

"You Mustn't Be Discouraged" HOPE and LOU

"The Dangerous Age" L.Z.

"The Fiddler and the Fighter" BYRON and ENSEMBLE

"Fade Out—Fade In" HOPE and RUDOLF

Finale THE COMPANY

Act One

SCENE ONE

In front of the F.F.F. gate. The gate is a large, wrought-iron affair, typical of many studios in the 1930's. The casual passer-by could peek through these gates into fairyland, but unless you possessed that magical piece of paper—"the movie contract"—you could never really hope to enter. It created a so-near-and-yet-so-far feeling for the panting young movie aspirants of the thirties who kept pouring into Hollywood by the thousands from all parts of the country.

Above the gate, at center, is the studio emblem—the picture of a seal, with the words emblazoned around it:

F.F.F. STUDIOS

The Seal of Approval

An aging, tough-looking studio cop is guarding the gate. There is a sign at one side, with an arrow pointing off left, which reads: Casting.

Several youngsters, seeking autographs, are standing near the gate, eyes eagerly peeled for the arrival of their idols. There is the bustle of morning activity as a mingling of outdoor-type and dress extras keep crossing and entering the gate. A couple of stars, who might conceivably be Bette Davis and Greta Garbo, leaving the studio, follow each other briskly through the gate, receiving obsequious salutes from the studio cop. Garbo slithers off anonymously, with head and hat pulled down. A star couple—obviously Nelson Eddy and Jeanette MacDonald—enter left; she is in dainty crinolines, he in Northwest Mounty uniform.

3

They approach the gate to enter and are stopped by the
AUTOGRAPH KIDS, *one of whom snaps their picture. Nelson
and Jeanette pose, blow a kiss to their fans, and continue
through the gate. From right a regal-looking actress enters
and crosses the gate.*

AUTOGRAPH KIDS   There she is! Helga Sixtrees!
(They run toward her, but she sweeps by)

COP *(Warmly, opening the gate)*   Good morning, Miss
Sixtrees . . .

HELGA *(Going through the gate)*   Good morning, Pops . . .

AUTOGRAPH KID *(Shouting after her)*   Helga, we love
you!
*(BILLY VESPERS comes from inside the gate. He is
the casting director—a busy-looking, beaming man
with a flower in his buttonhole. Behind him is
ROSCOE, the studio publicity man, carrying a camera
and a ladder)*

ROSCOE *(To the cop)*   Hi ya, Pops . . .
(He goes to set up the ladder)

POPS   Something special today, Mr. Vespers?

VESPERS *(Impatiently eying his watch)*   Yes . . . a new
girl coming out from New York to test . . . she should
be here any second now . . . A girl named Hope Springfield . . . some usherette in a Broadway movie house, I
understand . . . You all set, Roscoe?

4

ROSCOE (*Adjusting the camera*)   Right, Mr. Vespers. The usual?

VESPERS   Yes, yes . . . We'll do the ladder bit here by the gate . . .
   (*The* AUTOGRAPH KIDS *look off toward the right and rush in that direction*)

AUTOGRAPH KIDS   There he is! It's Byron! Byron Prong!
   (BYRON PRONG, *movie star, enters with* LYMAN, *his agent.* BYRON *looks dashing in a sport jacket and ascot, polo coat over his shoulders, and sunglasses. He creates an impression of sun-baked virility, but there is a look of excessive self-indulgence about him that suggests he will suddenly crumble one day into an instant old man*)

BYRON (*Stopping, talking angrily over his shoulder to* LYMAN *as he signs autograph books*)   I'm the studio's most valuable hunk of stuff . . . and they're going to rush me right from a prison epic into a musical! What kind of an agent are you?

LYMAN   Sweetie, that musical's gonna make history . . .

BYRON   I told you I wouldn't do it! Ruby Keeler and Alice Faye turned you down, didn't they?

AUTOGRAPH KID (*Kneeling to take a picture of* BYRON, *calls to him to look into the camera*)   Mr. Prong!
   (BYRON *turns his head, removes his sunglasses, and manages his most engaging smile, just as the picture is snapped. Then he turns it off instantly*)

5

LYMAN But, baby, they're getting you the greatest—
Ginger Rogers! It's all set!

BYRON (*With majestic rage, as he starts for the gate*) I
don't care! I'm going up to Lionel Z. Governor's office
right now and have a showdown!

LYMAN (*Following him, scared*) You can't do that, baby
. . . Anyway, L.Z.'s in Europe.

BYRON If I didn't know that, do you think I'd be talking
this way?
(*They both laugh and exit through the gate. REX,
a studio official, enters*)

REX (*Calling to VESPERS*) Billy!
(*At this point enter HOPE SPRINGFIELD—American
Girl. She is modestly attired, gawkily charming, and
always a little self-deprecatingly embarrassed—un-
sure of herself. She is far from ugly, but exactly
the opposite of Hollywood oomph and glamour. At
the moment she is terribly excited as she looks
around, wide-eyed with wonderment. A few feet
behind HOPE comes the studio CHAUFFEUR, carrying her suitcase. At the same time a female dress
extra enters, and goes to the gate and through it.
VESPERS, checking his notes, looks up and sees the
studio men. He goes to them, but passes right by
HOPE, who is staring up at the gate*)

VESPERS (*Panicky*) Rex . . . where's the girl? Did you
miss her at the station? Where's Hope Springfield?

REX What do you mean?

VESPERS The girl . . . Hope Springfield!
(HOPE *is standing close to the gate, to one side,
transfixed. Another pretty girl has entered from the
left and goes toward the gate, near* HOPE)

REX There she is . . . behind you!

VESPERS (*Turning*) Oh . . . Oh! (*He sees and goes toward the pretty girl*) Miss Springfield!

GIRL (*Looking puzzled*) Who?

VESPERS Aren't you Miss Springfield?
(*The* GIRL *smiles and shakes her head, then goes
through gate.* HOPE *takes a step or two toward*
VESPERS, *awkwardly*)

REX Billy . . . no—no! *That's* the one!
(*There is a harp effect from the orchestra, and a
pink spotlight focuses on* HOPE *for a moment*)

HOPE (*Shyly*) I'm Hope Springfield.

VESPERS (*Surprised, but covering up*) Oh . . . yes! Miss
Springfield, of *course!* (*He goes to her and shakes hands
with hearty enthusiasm*) I'm Billy Vespers, head of
talent. Mr. Lionel Z. Governor is on his way to Europe
or he would have been here to greet you himself! Well,
well, well! Welcome to F.F.F. Studios!

HOPE (*Gleeful*) Thank you! I'm *here!* Just a few days
ago I was an usher at the Strand Theatre, and now here
I am in Hollywood! Gee . . . I sure wish I could thank
Mr. Governor in person.

VESPERS   But . . . you've been seeing him, of course . . .

HOPE   Oh, no—I've never even met him!

VESPERS   I don't understand . . .

HOPE   Well, you see . . . it was at this world premiere of
L. Z. Governor's latest production . . . and all of us
ushers were lined up in the lobby to salute Mr. Governor
. . . but he couldn't stay . . . he had to catch a boat for
Europe. I saw him looking at us usherettes and then he
sort of counted, like . . . and then he dashed out! Later
his talent scout came back to our locker room and had
us girls line up like we were in the lobby . . . and guess
what . . . *Me!*

VESPERS   You were the one, eh? Well, well, well . . .

HOPE   Nobody could believe it. The girl in line next to
me—Gloria Currie—she claimed he was smiling at her
the whole time. Boy, was she surprised! Everybody was
surprised—even my mother!

VESPERS   Miss Springfield . . . before we go in . . . I'd
like to get a picture of you right here at the gate . . .
(*He starts to take her to where* ROSCOE *has set up a ladder near the wall*) All right, Roscoe . . .

ROSCOE   (*Wielding a camera*)   Hold that!
        (*Two* COWBOY EXTRAS *enter*)

HOPE   (*Sees* COWBOY EXTRAS)   Hey! Look . . . a movie
star!

8

VESPERS (*Looks up*) Where?

HOPE (*Excited, points at them*) There!

VESPERS Oh, those are just extras . . .

HOPE Excuse me . . . (*She goes to one of the* COWBOY EXTRAS. *The other continues in through gate*) Uh . . . I beg your pardon . . .

FIRST COWBOY EXTRA (*An especially rugged type*) Um-hm?

HOPE Are you an extra?

FIRST COWBOY EXTRA Mm-hm.

HOPE But you're Bronco McClure—my favorite silent cowboy star! What happened?

FIRST COWBOY EXTRA (*With a thick British accent*) Ah don't quate know, rahlly . . .
(*He crosses and exits through the gate*)

VESPERS How on earth did you recognize him?

HOPE (*Bubbling*) Oh, I know all his movies backwards. You see, my mother was an usher and my father was a projectionist—in Jackson Heights. I was almost born during *Birth of a Nation* . . . (*She looks off left*) Look! George Hackaway—silent gangster star! (GANGSTER EXTRA, *smoking a cigarette, hat pulled down, scurries in from the left.* HOPE *runs excitedly to him*) Excuse me, sir . . . but aren't you George Hackaway, silent gangster star?

GANGSTER EXTRA   Thweetie . . . I'm thorry . . . but I'm in a dethperate hurry!
(*He dashes off, exiting through the gate*)

HOPE   He was the greatest!

VESPERS   And now . . . we'd like to get a picture of you with the F.F.F. trademark . . .
(*He leads her over to the ladder, where* ROSCOE *is waiting with the camera*)

HOPE (*Looking up at the emblem*)   The seal!
(*She climbs the ladder, and sings "It's Good to Be Back Home"*)
How often I've stood at the back of the theatre,
Watching the M.G.M. lion . . .
(*She roars, turning toward the camera as* ROSCOE *snaps a picture*)
And how well I got to know
The Pathé rooster's crow
And Warner Brothers' "W.B."
(*She gestures with two hands, making the emblem come toward the camera*)
And the R.K.O. signal
(*She makes the signal as she comes down from the ladder*)
"Beebeebeebeebeebeebeebeeeeep . . ."
And the F.F.F. trademark—
"F.F.F. presents . . .
(*Speaks*)

The Seal of Approval!"
    (*She does three seal barks and a flippers gesture*)
This town is full of such familiar sights and scenes,
From a life of seeing movies
And reading fan magazines.

I've never been here before, but it's good to be back
        home.
I've never been here before and yet
It makes me cry to see those old familiar faces.
Wherever my eyes turn,
I see friends galore.
And though they don't know me,
I know them—you see,
None of them knows
I met them at Loew's!
I'm new here in Hollywood, but I'm proud of my
        home town.
I can't wait until I beat my feet
On Vine and Sunset—all those old familiar places.
To me the Brown Derby
Beats St. Peter's Dome . . .
I should say "Hollywood, I'll lick you yet, I'll beat
        you!"
But I don't care—I'm just so thrilled to get to meet
        you . . .
I've never been here before, but it's good to be back
        home!"
    (*As* HOPE *turns to follow* VESPERS *and* POPS *through
    the gate, both gate and wall open up to reveal . . .*)

Scene Two

The studio lot. We see sound stages marked by various numbers, and large pieces of scenery standing about the area. As hope *walks around, she is completely overcome by an ecstasy that is pure Alice in Wonderland. An entire cross section of Hollywood dances around her and seems to welcome her as she joins in with them. She dances and kicks with a large assortment of Busby Berkley-ish hooferettes, as Mae West, Bette Davis, Merle Oberon, Nelson Eddy and Jeanette MacDonald, Greta Garbo, and Jean Harlow parade by, looking their most glamorous and characteristic. She is happily intertangled dancing with Dracula, Tarzan, Louis XVI and Marie Antoinette, Fred Astaire and Ginger Rogers, and Harpo, Chico and Groucho Marx. As they dance off, she resumes singing.*

HOPE

> I've never been here before, but it's good to be back
>   home.
> I've never been here before and yet
> It makes me cry to see those old familiar faces.
> To me every palm tree
> Tops the pines of Rome!
> It's good to be back,
> It's good to be back—
> I've never been here before, but it's good to be . . .
> Back home!

(*She is left alone on stage, high and exhilarated, as she finishes. Then* VESPERS *enters from the left, beckons to her, and she dashes out after him. As the lights fade, the set revolves to . . .*)

Scene Three

The executive dining room. There is a long dining table, around which are seated the nephews of L.Z. Governor— there are six of them, and they are all vice-presidents. At center, on a paneled wall-section hangs an impressive portrait of L.Z. Governor himself, dominating the scene. In the center of the table is a big red chair—more like a throne, really. And above the portrait, sculptured into the paneling, the F.F.F. seal and emblem.

One nephew, RUDOLF, *is unlike the others. Earnest, youthful, he sits at the right end of the table.* RALPH, *another nephew, is a portly, well-fed-looking man of about forty, with a sly, foxy expression—he is pompous and filled with self-importance. He sits in the chair to the left of "the throne." There are dessert plates in front of each man, and they are eating as the set revolves into place.*

ROSCOE (*Standing to one side, with his assistants*) Gentlemen, we need a decision on the title for the Huckleberry Finn picture. Is it *Mississippi Days*—or *Mississippi Nights?*

RALPH (*Rising*) Never mind that, Roscoe! (*He addresses them all*) My dear cousins, and fellow vice-presidents . . . Our beloved chief, Uncle Lionel, has just written me a letter. It's from Vienna . . . (*He pulls the letter out of his pocket and waves it importantly*) He wrote to *me* because he has sent a new discovery out here and won't be back in time to greet her himself—(*Reading from the letter*) "My latest personal discovery . . . I picked her from a line of usherettes at the Strand Theatre . . . she has everything . . . Got me in the gut!"

GEORGE (*Complaining*) I don't see why he should write just to you. Frank's the oldest.

FRANK You're only Nephew Number Four, Ralph . . .

RALPH (*Smugly*) But I'm his heir apparent! He still calls you boys by number . . . You're not Frank—you're Nephew Number One. And you're Nephew Number Three. He's stopped calling me Number Four! He just says . . . "Good morning, Ralph" . . . "Good evening, Ralph" . . .

RUDOLF I also heard him say, "What the hell are you doing there, Ralph?"

RALPH (*Sitting*) When was that?

RUDOLF The day you accidentally sat in his chair. And you're doing it again! (RALPH *looks around a second. Sure enough, he is sitting on Uncle Lionel's throne— and he jumps up as if shot.* RUDOLF *chuckles*) Maybe I will tell Uncle Lionel.

RALPH (*Defiantly*) You wouldn't dare. You wouldn't commit yourself on anything around this studio.

RUDOLF So true.

RALPH (*Sneering*) A genuine coward, aren't you, Rudolf?

RUDOLF   That I'll commit myself on. Yes!
        (*He sings "Fear"*)
    Ralph, we'd never tell on you,
    And we'd like to feel you'd never tell on us.
    What is it that makes us all true-blue?
    What holds us together like glue?

ALL (*Singing—a heroic-sounding marching tune*)
    Fear . . . simple fear!
    That's the tie that binds us
    All together . . .

RUDOLF
    Here . . . it is clear . . . we're in fear!

A NEPHEW
    We live in mortal terror
    That we'll commit an error
    And though we seem so firmly rooted,

ALL
    We can suddenly be booted
    Out on our ear . . .

RUDOLF
    We're cowards!

ALL
    Fear . . . grisly fear!
    That's the truth that finds us
    Shouting "All for one,
    One for all!"
    All the year . . .

16

Since our employment seems to any normal person—
Incomprehensible,

RUDOLF

We spend our time trying to look
Utterly indispensable.

ALL

So let's lift our glasses and cheer
The strongest union out here—
The brotherhood of fear!
(*At the conclusion of this bravura song,* VESPERS
enters through the door, with HOPE *shyly following*)

VESPERS Mr. Governor . . . Mr. Governor . . .

RALPH Yes, what is it, Vespers?

VESPERS Mr. Ralph . . . I'd like you to meet someone the
studio just signed—

RALPH (*Cutting in, impatiently*) Look, Vespers . . . we
haven't time to meet every bit player on the lot!

VESPERS But, gentlemen . . . gentlemen. This is Hope
Springfield. Lionel Z. Governor's *personal discovery!*
(*The harp effect is heard again, and the angelic spot
focuses on* HOPE. RALPH *turns to her—his attitude
and that of the others suddenly transformed*)

RALPH (*Shaking hands with* HOPE, *effusively sincere*)
Miss Springfield . . . I am Ralph Governor, vice-president
in charge of production. (*As he introduces each nephew,*

17

each man goes to HOPE, *shakes her hand, and returns to his chair*) This is Frank Governor, vice-president in charge of distribution . . . George Governor, vice-president in charge of publicity . . . Harold Governor, vice-president in charge of budget . . . Arnold Governor, vice-president in charge of foreign market . . . and Rudolf, vice-president in charge of approval.

HOPE   How do you do?

RUDOLF (*Stares at her for a moment, then drops her hand and turns to* RALPH)   But this girl isn't Uncle Lionel's type at all!

HOPE (*Startled and hurt. Faintly*)   What do you mean?

RALPH   What did you say?

RUDOLF (*Sorry he said it*)   I said she's not his type.
          (*The nephews turn on him, aghast.* HOPE *looks at him with surprise and displeasure*)

RALPH (*Jumping on him*)   Rudolf! You're questioning L.Z.'s taste? Yes or no?

RUDOLF (*Retreating deftly*)   Look, Ralph, I didn't say I *didn't like* her type . . . I only said she's a different type from Uncle Lionel's type, which has up till now been more of a floozie type. But this is a more wholesome, girl-next-door type!

HOPE (*Truly insulted*)   What an awful thing to say!

RALPH (*Goes to* HOPE, *moving* RUDOLF *away*) Miss Springfield, don't mind Mr. Rudolf. What he says doesn't matter.

HOPE   But he's in charge of approval . . .

RALPH   Approval is our seal's name. He buys fish for the seal.

HOPE   Oh.

RALPH   We have a letter from L.Z. (*Reads from L.Z.'s letter*) "Test for female lead in new musical comedy . . . opposite Byron Prong."

HOPE (*Almost swooning*) Byron Prong! I never even thought I'd get to *meet* him!

RALPH (*Decisively; he seems to be taking over*) You can meet him right now. (*To* ROSCOE) Get Byron Prong up here at once! He's on Stage One, right next door . . .
   (ROSCOE *runs out the door*)

HOPE (*Frantically*) But—my hair!
   (*She clutches her head*)

RALPH (*Pointing the way offstage*) Right in here, Miss Springfield . . .

HOPE (*Hurrying out, gesturing gratitude*) Oh, thank you!
   (*The nephews look at one another nervously*)

HAROLD (*To* RALPH) Are you sure—

19

RALPH (*With an insincere chuckle*) Let's show Uncle Lionel we are capable of carrying on just as if he were here . . .
>
> (*The nephews look terrified*)

ROSCOE (*Entering through the door*) Byron Prong!
> (*Through the door come five men—grizzled and unshaven—in striped convict uniforms of the period . . . they walk lumberingly, in step, their ankles chained together. The last convict in line carries an iron ball. All their faces are blackened with dirt . . . but the fourth one in line is* BYRON PRONG, *hard to recognize*)

BYRON (*Angrily—almost hysterical*) All right, now what the hell is this! We're in the middle of shooting the escape scene. They didn't even take the time to unlock us!

RALPH (*Ignoring* BYRON's *wrath*) Byron . . . we've seen the rushes on this picture you're shooting—*The Fugitive Steps Out*—and if you're not an Oscar winner . . . then I don't know anything!

BYRON Okay, so I'm not an Oscar winner. Is that what you got me up here for? We're trying to finish the picture by tomorrow!

RALPH Well, you know your next picture is a musical . . . and do you know who your new leading lady may be?

BYRON Yeah . . . Ginger Rogers.

RALPH (*Extravagantly*) Ginger Rogers! Who needs her! Skinny little boys like Fred Astaire! We're trying to get you . . . Hope Springfield!

BYRON (*Blankly*) Who?
(HOPE *re-enters, tentatively—looking exactly the same*)

RALPH Hope Springfield!

HOPE (*Timidly*) Yes?

RALPH (*Gesturing*) She's here to test with you! She's L.Z.'s personal discovery. (HOPE *wipes lipstick from her teeth as* RALPH *brings her toward the chain gang*) Hope . . . this is Byron Prong!

HOPE (*With great certainty, to the last convict—the wrong man*) Oh, Mr. Prong, just a few days ago I was talking about you with some girls in our locker room in New York . . . and now I'm *here* . . . talking to you in person! Oh, Mr. Prong . . . you could be in prison stripes . . . or made up like the Hunchback of Notre Dame—or King Kong! You're still the most beautiful man in the world!
(*She is looking intently into the convict's face as* BYRON *whips off his dirty hat, gives it to the convict, seizes the iron ball proudly, and flashes his profile*)

BYRON *I* am Byron Prong!

HOPE (*With a hysterical giggle as she sees her mistake*) Oh-h-h! (*Collecting herself*) Oh, Mr. Prong—I'm sorry

21

—I'm just so *nervous!* I just can't get over the fact that I'm going to be appearing opposite *you* in a screen test!

RALPH Well, I think Miss Springfield ought to get settled right away. This letter from L.Z. says she's to be set up in the—uh—starlet bungalow.

RUDOLF (*Stepping forward nervously*) The bungalow? ... Her?

RALPH (*Sniffing for a sign of mutiny*) Any objections?

RUDOLF Uh . . . Why should I object? I'd just like to volunteer to escort Miss Springfield over to the bungalow . . . (*He takes* HOPE's *arm*) Let's go, Miss Springfield!

HOPE (*Her eyes still on* BYRON, *who is staring away from her haughtily*) Oh! Uh—well, goodbye for now, Mr. Prong. Could I—could I have your autograph?
    (*She clumsily fishes an autograph book from her purse*)

BYRON (*With great control*) Certainly.
    (*He hands* HOPE *the heavy iron ball he's been holding. She almost plummets through the floor, but manages to hold it bravely while he signs her book. They exchange ball and book*)

HOPE Oh, thank you—thank you! (*She exits with* RUDOLF, *falling all over herself in joyous confusion as she goes*) Sorry!
    (*And she is gone*)

BYRON (*Turning to the executives in a rage*)   Listen, you
apes! (*As he steps toward them threateningly, he is first
yanked backward by his chains, then drags the other
four convicts after him as he talks*) I have played opposite Greta Garbo, Claudette Colbert, Joan Blondell . . .
and I have made them all look good! But I am *not* going
to play opposite Rebecca of Sunnybrook Farm!

RALPH (*Bluntly*)   You'll play opposite Minnie Mouse if
L.Z. says so. Or this studio may be forced to stop paying
off your gambling debt . . . which is approximately $250-
000 at the moment!

BYRON (*Making a lightning-fast adjustment*)   That's what
I said. The girl is great. You can tell L.Z. I think the
girl is . . . *great*. (*Speaks*) Fear! Simple fear!
    (*Sings*)
  Is the tie that binds me.
  It's as plain as day
  I must play
  What they say.
  With gambling debts to pay off
  I can't afford a layoff,
  So if they say "Play Tarzan's mother,"
  Tarzan's mother and no other,
  That's what I play . . .
  They've got me!

ALL (*Marching in place*)
  Fear—
      Nothing but fear—
  Grisly fear—

The grisliest fear—
That's the truth—
The awfullest truth—
That finds us . . .

BYRON

Compromising . . .

ALL

Year after year after year after year after year!
It's all for none and none for all—
We're frightened and afraid.

BYRON

Each day we learn whose heads have rolled
By simply reading *Daily Variety*.
Where else on earth can you combine
Sunshine and such anxiety?

ALL

We're the strongest union out here . . .

BYRON

The brotherhood of . . .
(*A voice from offstage shouts: "Byron Prong—on the set!"* BYRON *instinctively starts to obey, yanking all the other convicts with him. They are entangled in their chains, then they stop and turn to bravely sing the final, definitive word*)

ALL

FEAR!
(*The lights fade as they are revolved out of sight*)

24

Scene Four

The wardrobe department. There is a hubbub of mid-day activity as MYRA, *a wardrobe mistress in her sixties, and a younger seamstress are fitting the gown of* HELGA SIX-TREES, *who stands on a small fitting platform. Several girl dancers in new costumes are trying out dance steps near a small folding screen. In the background is a drop depicting rows and rows of hanging costumes, and at left is a rack with dresses hanging on it, and a wardrobe table. Several more extras in French Revolution costumes stand about, casually.* RUDOLF *is perched on one end of the wardrobe table, patiently waiting.*

VESPERS (*Entering*) All right—French Revolution . . . They're ready for you on Stage Thirteen! (*The extras take their flags and muskets and march out left*) Is Hope Springfield all set in the bungalow, Mr. Rudolf?

RUDOLF Oh, yes . . .

VESPERS (*Has checked his notes and dismissed several dancing girls; they exit with* MYRA *following after them*) Miss Sixtrees . . . they're waiting for you . . .

SIXTREES Coming, for God's sake!
    (*She steps down off the fitting platform and starts to exit left. The seamstress follows along on her*

knees, still frantically pinning SIXTREES' *hem as she goes*)

VESPERS (*Checking his watch*) Miss Springfield's due over at make-up now . . .

RUDOLF I know . . . but she's still here being fitted . . . (VESPERS *exits, shaking his head, as* RUDOLF *calls toward the screen*) Miss Springfield—are you still in there?

HOPE (*Behind the screen*) Yes . . . I'm—I'm here!
        (*She sounds distressed*)

RUDOLF They're waiting for you . . . Come on out!

HOPE (*Still behind the screen*) I don't want to—I'm not quite ready!

RUDOLF What's holding you up?

HOPE Not much . . .
        (*She emerges from behind the screen. She is in an exotic, semi-nude outfit consisting mainly of strings of huge pearls, loosely draped. With every step she takes, they shake and clatter like a thunderstorm.* HOPE *looks uncomfortable and embarrassed, ludicrously trying to cover herself with her hands*)

RUDOLF (*Stunned*) My God!

HOPE (*Belligerently*) I suppose you're going to say I *still* look like the girl next door!

RUDOLF (*Gulping*) It all depends on the neighborhood! What picture can they be testing you for?

HOPE *Little Women?*

RUDOLF Well, I guess we ought to go. We can cut through the studio restaurant . . .

HOPE (*In a panic*) No. I'm not going to parade around like this . . . in broad daylight!

RUDOLF Why not? You've been telling me what a wicked life you lead back in New York . . . and what a woman of the world you are.

HOPE (*Considering this, she decides to try it, and swaggers a few steps across the stage—but the swinging and clatter of the pearls are too much for her. She stops and clutches at them*) No! You've made me feel self-conscious! *You're* the one who said I'm not the movie type. I agree with you. That's why I don't like you.

RUDOLF (*Removing his suit jacket*) Here, put this on.

HOPE (*Putting on his jacket*) Now I suppose I look like the *boy* next door!
    (MYRA *enters from right, carrying a few costumes*)

MYRA Hope Springfield?

RUDOLF Oh, Myra . . . this is Hope Springfield.

MYRA Oh . . . how do you do?

HOPE   Hey . . . aren't you Myra May Melrose?

MYRA   Yes, dear. Mr. Ralph just called. He wants you to wait on the set. So you're Hope Springfield, huh? (*Exiting right*) Well . . . ours not to reason why . . .

HOPE   Myra May Melrose! She was "America's Darling"! Rudolf, you don't know how lucky you are to be around people like that every day!

RUDOLF   It doesn't mean anything to me. I never saw her movies. I never go to the movies.

HOPE   You don't? How can you work out here and not care about movies?

RUDOLF   You *do*, don't you? You ought to see the look on your face right now . . . you look like a little girl . . .

HOPE   (*With mounting rage*)   You're saying it again, aren't you?

RUDOLF   What?

HOPE   That I'm about as exciting as a bowl of oatmeal.

RUDOLF   I *like* oatmeal!

HOPE   (*Defiantly*)   Oh, what do you know about me? The things I've seen and done—the life I've led!
      (*Sings "Call Me Savage"*)
   You don't know what to call me—
   You only just met me.

Check with all the ruined men back East
And you will find—
They can't forget me!
Call me savage,
Call me passion's child,
Call me wicked,
Uncontrolled and wild,
Call me Circe
With no mercy,
Call me deadly
Siren's medley.
Call me Cleo,
Call me Lorelei,
Call me Lilith,
Call me Evil Eye,
Mata Hari
Or DuBarry
Or Salome
Or don't know me!

RUDOLF (*Sings*)
    You're so sweet,
    So sort of helpless and petite,
    The kind that mothers like to meet—
    So pure and wholesome.
    I'll respect you,
    I'll protect you.

HOPE
    Call me lethal,
    Call me devilish,
    Call me toothsome,

Some delicious dish—
Call me savage—
You just gotta,
Or you're not a—
No, you're not a friend.

RUDOLF

I cannot . . .
Call you savage,
Call you passion's child,
Call you wicked,
Uncontrolled and wild,
Call you Circe
With no mercy—
You're no deadly
Siren's medley.
Call you Cleo,
Call you Lorelei,
Call you Lilith,
Call you Evil Eye,
Mata Hari
Or DuBarry,
Or Salome—
You're so homey.

HOPE

I'm not sweet.
Don't say I'm helpless and petite,
The kind that mothers like to meet—
Not pure and wholesome—
Don't respect me,
Don't protect me.

HOPE	RUDOLF
Call me lethal,	Call you lethal,
Call me devilish,	Call you devilish,
Call me toothsome,	Call you toothsome,
Some delicious dish,	Some delicious dish,
Call me savage!	
You just gotta—	Do I gotta?
Or you're not a—	Guess I'm not a—
No, you're not a . . .	No, I'm not a . . .
friend!	friend!

(*As she sings "Call Me Savage,"* HOPE *keeps posturing and parading about in a* femme fatale *manner that is highly energetic but totally unconvincing.* RUDOLF *is only amused by her frantic determination to appear wicked and worldly. Finally, ensnarled in her costume of wildly waving pearls, she gives up and collapses on the fitting platform in a disconsolate heap.* MYRA *enters from the right, as* RALPH *rushes in from the left*)

RALPH (*Highly excited*) Hold everything! Miss Springfield . . . Miss Springfield! (*Calling offstage*) Custer! Custer! (CUSTER CORKLEY *enters from left—he is a worried man, attired in beret, riding pants, and whip*) Miss Springfield . . . this is our great director-choreographer, Custer Corkley.

HOPE Oh—How do you do?

RALPH (*Expansively*) Uncle Lionel has just sent me a cable that he will be away for a whole month . . . and in his absence, I am taking over! Let's show him we don't need him . . . Let's make the picture!

31

CORKLEY (*Appalled*)   But I haven't even seen a script!

RALPH   Miss Springfield, I am putting you in the picture. You start shooting in the morning.

HOPE   You mean—I'm *in*? (*Incredulous*) I'm in the picture? And I don't even have to have a screen test?

RALPH   That's right! I want you to start studying this right away . . . (*Hands her a script*) It's a scene from *The Fiddler and the Fighter*.

HOPE (*Excited*)   *The Fiddler and the Fighter* . . . Which one do I play?

RALPH   The fiddler . . . a lady violinist.

HOPE (*Reading from the cast page with ecstatic delight*) Oh, yes, I see—"Griselda Swann . . . a great lady violinist . . . Hope Springfield." "Kid Bercovici . . . a rugged male fighter . . . Byron Prong!" Oh, Mr. Ralph . . . (*Tentatively*) What scene do I wear *this* in?
(*She opens her jacket—briefly—for him to see her costume*)

RALPH (*Aghast*)   Wrong costume! Get her out of it. Myra . . . what was that supposed to be for?

MYRA   *The Farmer and the Fan Dancer.*

RALPH (*Exploding*)   *The Fiddler and the Fighter!* Incompetence! Incompetence! Hope . . . (*Taking her hand*) Get a good night's rest—it's the last you'll have for quite a while. We've got a picture to shoot!

(*He exits.* MYRA *has helped* HOPE *into a dressing gown, and she returns the jacket to* RUDOLF. MYRA *exits with the costumes as* CORKLEY *exits with a smile and a wave to* HOPE)

HOPE (*Clutching the script to her*)   Oh, Rudolf . . . Just think! Only a few days ago I was just an usherette. Now I'm in the picture! Opposite Byron Prong! (*Taking a pose*) I am Griselda Swann! (*She goes to* RUDOLF *and extends her hand*) Wish me luck?

RUDOLF (*Taking her hand—warmly*)   Good luck . . . savage.

(*He exits.* HOPE, *left alone, hugs the script to her and sings with quiet wonderment* "*The Usher from the Mezzanine*")

The usher from the mezzanine
Will soon be seen on the silver screen,
On the screen she once used to stare at five shows a
    day.
The usher's face in black and white
Will fill the screen every day and night,
And a million ushers will stare at her the same way.
So don't give up, all you short or fat or tall girls.
Democracy says fame can come to all girls!
Is there a girl with soul so dead
Who never once to herself has said
I could make it, too, if I had the chance to be seen?
Do I want it?
Yes, I want it!
So watch your local screen
For the usher from the mezzanine.

(*As the lights fade, the set revolves to* . . .)

Scene Five

On the set, there are pieces of scenery strewn about. A
light bridge is visible overhead, banked with spotlights,
workmen wander about carrying electrical equipment, a
few canvas deck chairs are placed at the right and near
these a painter on a ladder puts finishing touches on a drop.
The set is bustling with the activity of a large sound stage
in action.

In one corner RALPH, VESPERS and CORKLEY are busily
conferring with MAX WELCH, author of the screenplay,
The Fiddler and the Fighter. Mr. Welch is a harassed,
sloppily dressed little man. At center stage, dancers in rehearsal clothes are practicing a routine, to a thumping piano
accompaniment, that obviously has been going on for hours.
BYRON PRONG, standing near the upright piano, in dressing
gown with a towel around his neck, is singing an epically
lilting waltz—he is working diligently and is obviously
pleased with his vocal efforts. The expression on his face
conveys the passionate finesse of a great performing artist in
his shining hour.

BYRON (Sings "My Heart Is Like a Violin")
> My heart is like a violin . . .
> A tune comes out when you come in.
> You smile and then the strings begin
> A tune that's gay—
> Some gay roundelay . . .
> Ah, but when you frown,

34

Feeling down,
Then the gay
Roundelay
Starts fading.
A violin is like my heart . . .
Without your touch the beat won't start.
And if you ever should depart,
My heart's so gen-
Tle an instrument
That the strings would break
For your sake—
So beware,
Have a care!
Unlike some,
It's not a drum
Or balalaika . . .
My heart's like a
Violin.

CORKLEY (*Very excited, calling out orders*)   All right! All
you violin girls and bow boys . . . take ten!
> (*The piano accompaniment stops abruptly as the
> dancers break and stand talking in groups*)

BYRON (*To the girl at the piano*)   Hit it again, Bertha.
(*Sings*)
> My heart is like a violin . . .
> A tune comes out when you come in.
> > (*During this,* RALPH *has taken* CORKLEY *aside. He
> > whispers something into* CORKLEY's *ear, pointing at*
> > BYRON, *then* RALPH *begins to leave the set, clapping*
> > BYRON *warmly on the shoulder as he passes him.
> > Then, as soon as* RALPH *has exited*)

CORKLEY (*Sharply*)   Okay, Byron . . . *Cut!* (BYRON *dwindles off impatiently*) That song's out of the picture!

BYRON (*As if struck by lightning*)   What? But we can't lose that song, Corkley! It's got some of my best notes! It's —just listen, Corkley! (*Sings a cappella*) My heart is like a violin . . .

CORKLEY (*Firmly*)   It's out, Byron. Mr. Ralph's orders!
    (BYRON *continues to mouth the words and sing very softly, almost weeping, as* HOPE, RALPH, MYRA *and* RUDOLF *enter the set. Then he retires to a corner, disconsolately*)

RALPH (*Bringing* HOPE *to the center*)   Miss Springfield, I'd like you to meet the author of the screenplay, Max Welch . . .
    (WELCH *steps forward*)

HOPE (*Shaking his hand*)   How do you do?

RALPH (*Stepping forward, taking over*)   All right, everyone. Boys and girls—this is the new leading lady of *The Fiddler and the Fighter* . . . Hope Springfield! (*The others on the set applaud politely, as* HOPE *smiles furtively*) As this is our first day of shooting, I would like to say that *The Fiddler and the Fighter* is like a great ship we are launching on the stormy seas of production. Let's surprise L.Z. Governor on his return with our ship safely back at home plate! Let's get to work!

CORKLEY   All right—let's sit down. (CORKLEY, HOPE *and* WELCH *take seats on the deck chairs grouped together.*

RALPH, MYRA, VESPERS, BYRON *and* RUDOLF *find chairs or platforms to sit on. Some dancers drift off, right and left)* Right from the top!

HOPE *(Reading from her script)* *The Fiddler and the Fighter* . . . original story idea by Max Welch. Screenplay by Aldous Huxley, William Faulkner, and F. Scott Fitzgerald. Additional dialogue by W. Somerset Maugham, Thomas Mann and Fannie Hurst. Final screenplay by Max Welch.

CORKLEY *(Eying the script)* Looks pretty thin for a full script.

HOPE Well—all we've been given so far is this one scene.

RALPH *(Exploding)* That's all?

WELCH *(Sweating, turns to RALPH)* At the moment, that's all there is.

RALPH *(Alarmed)* We have to have a picture to shoot!

WELCH I'll have it—I'm having a little plot trouble.

HOPE Really, Mr. Welch, I can't see why.

WELCH *(Turning to her)* How's that?

HOPE Well, from just this one scene—between the rugged male pugilist and the long-haired girl violinist—the whole story was perfectly clear to me.

WELCH   Yeah? What is it?

HOPE   Well, as Kid Bercovici says in the scene to Griselda Swann . . . well, he feels that their worlds can never meet. So the story must be that he's from the Lower East Side and he thinks she's upper crust, but then he finds out that she was once poor, too, and before she got famous she studied violin with the Federal Music Project . . . on the WPA. And then of course, it's all about putting on this big show.

WELCH (*Has taken out a pad and pencil*)   Of course . . . Go on.

HOPE   Well, it's this big benefit for the wives and kiddies of boxers who lost all their money in the stock market crash. She's going to be in the show with him . . . long hair and jazz getting together like . . .

WELCH (*Writing*)   Not bad!

HOPE   . . . and he's promised her he'll give up boxing. But at the last minute some gangsters cheat him, and he hasn't got enough money to put on the show. He can't tell her why . . . but he has to box again to raise the money. And she's furious!

CORKLEY (*Breathless*)   Then what?

HOPE   Well, naturally she's going to show *him* . . . so the same night he's boxing in Madison Square Garden, she gets herself booked to play the concerto in Carnegie

Hall. (*She rises, begins to act it out feverishly*) Shot! We see Madison Square Garden . . . he's losing the fight . . . his heart isn't in it 'cause she's left him. Pam! Pam! Pow! Cut to Carnegie Hall . . . she's playing the concerto. Cut back to the Garden . . . Ow! Ugh! Cut back to Carnegie . . . Eeeooo eeeooo eeeooo! (*Playing the violin*) At a break in the violin part she rushes to the wings to listen to the radio . . . and she hears the report come over . . . (*In fight announcer's voice*) Kid Bercovici is being slaughtered . . . He's *down!* One! Two! Three! Cut to the Garden . . . (*Acting the referee*) The count is six! Seven! . . . We see Griselda running down the aisle of Madison Square Garden to the ringside . . . (*She runs in place*) She lifts her violin and starts playing . . . their song! (*Pantomimes fraught violin playing*) We see his head . . . shaken . . . groggy . . . Eight! A blurred shot of her face from his angle . . . suddenly it's clear . . . She's *there!* The count is *nine* . . . he's up on his feet. She is playing away . . . (*Sawing feverishly*) And then we see the entire Philharmonic Orchestra from Carnegie Hall flooding down the aisles of Madison Square Garden . . .

WELCH (*Writing furiously*)   Great!

HOPE (*With passionate intensity*) They followed her there, and they're playing with her! He's up on his feet good now! Wham! Pam! A right to the chin . . . and his opponent Bull Montana is down for the count of ten. He pulls her up into the ring, his hand is raised . . . they kiss . . . and we dissolve through to the big Boxer Benefit, where we see thousands of people screaming in the audience. (WELCH *rises*) The big finale is just about to begin . . . (*In her enthusiasm, she shoves* WELCH *back into his chair*) but the main girl and boy singer have been drugged by the gangsters . . . so Kid and Griselda have to go on in their places, and they sing this great song about how this country is recovering and finding itself again and whether you're a fiddler or a fighter . . . you're first and foremost—an American!

    (*She claps hand over her heart and collapses into her chair. Everyone on the set applauds excitedly, as* WELCH *rises with his notebook and goes to* RALPH)

WELCH   You know what? That's exactly the story I've been working on.

RALPH   Of course it is. Congratulations, Welch . . . it's great! And remember . . . let's go all out on your patriotic finale. There'll never be another depression . . . and there'll never be another war! The Mussolinis and the Hitlers—they've got their problems, but that's over *there* . . . we're over *here* . . . and the blue eagle of recovery is spreading its wings over us all . . . and et cetera. Get all that into the finale . . . but keep it sexy!

    (RALPH, CORKLEY *and* VESPERS *hold a conference with* WELCH *at the left, as* RUDOLF *approaches* HOPE *tentatively, kneeling beside her chair*)

RUDOLF (*Shyly*) You know . . . you must have hypnotized me. Your enthusiasm . . . I ran some old movies last night—

HOPE (*Lighting up*) Really?

RUDOLF One Garbo . . . two Chaplins . . . I—(*Just then* BYRON *walks past them;* HOPE *looks at him, forgetting* RUDOLF) I'm getting hold of the Marx Brothers in *Monkey Business* . . . I hoped maybe you'd watch it with me when . . .

CORKLEY Well, we've got a scene and a number . . . so let's get them on their feet . . . (WELCH, VESPERS *and* RALPH *exit left.* RUDOLF *rises and sits at one side to watch*) Now, Hope, the scene is—as you know—Kid Bercovici's training camp . . . before your entrance, the Kid is working out, and has a scene with his man Friday . . . (*Looks around, then calls offstage*) Call Lou Williams!
    (*A colored actor wearing a robe enters*)

LOU (*Pleasant, normal speech*) Right here, Mr. Corkley . . .

CORKLEY Hope Springfield, this is Lou Williams . . .

HOPE (*Shaking hands with* LOU) Oh, hi! I'm a big fan of yours . . .

LOU Thanks. Good luck on your first day.

HOPE Thank you!

CORKLEY Byron! You and Lou run these first few lines . . . right here . . .
    (MYRA *takes* HOPE *offstage for a costume change.*

BYRON *takes the script from* CORKLEY *. . . both* BYRON *and* LOU *read from the script in casual monotones—for lines, not expression*)

LOU   "Mr. Bercovici—"

BYRON   "Yes, what is it, Lightning?"

LOU   "There's a lady outside . . . kind of wants to see you."

BYRON   "I told you I didn't want to see anybody."

LOU   "I told her that, but then I noticed she had a machine gun with her."

BYRON   "A machine gun?"

CORKLEY   That's enough. Lou, I don't have to tell you what you're supposed to do in this scene . . .

LOU   The usual, Mr. Corkley?

CORKLEY   The usual . . .
(BYRON *moves to rehearsal area. He takes off robe and begins to flex muscles, do breathing exercises, and pantomime workout with a punching bag*)

CORKLEY (*Sitting in the director's chair, facing them*)   Rehearsal! Quiet, everyone! . . . Okay, Byron. Enter Lou!
(BYRON *goes into action with the punching bag.* LOU *has taken off his robe and put script down. He is revealed in tattered shirt, overalls with suspenders*

and large floppy shoes. He shuffles toward BYRON,
slouching . . . mouth hanging, eyes bugging out—
Willie Best, Stepin Fetchit style)

LOU (*Deep South, mumbling*) "Mmmmmmmmmmm-
mmmmsah Buhkoveechee . . ."

BYRON (*Stops punching*) "Yes, what is it, Lightning?"

LOU "Dey's a lady out sahde . . . kahnda wonts to see
ya . . ."

BYRON "I told you I didn't want to see anybody . . ."

LOU "Ah tol huh dat . . . but den Ah notice she had a
machine gun wid huh . . ."

BYRON "A machine gun?"

LOU "She's carryin' a vah-o-lin case . . . and dat kin oney
mean one thing . . . (*He holds up two fingers, then only
one*) . . . dere's a machine gun insahde! Ah could feel
de wings sproutin' outa mah back riaht den an' dere . . .
Ah ain't ready fo' no green pastures just yit, boss . . ."
(*He exits shuffling and mumbling, receives an
"okay" sign from* CORKLEY *as he finishes, then
straightens up, puts on his robe, and sits at one
side*)

CORKLEY Okay. Let's run Miss Springfield's entrance,
now. (HOPE *re-enters with* MYRA, *who has helped her
change into a white raincoat and a slouch hat. She carries a prop violin case, as she nervously approches* BY-
RON) Hope, you come in right from there.

43

(BYRON, *as the Kid, does deep-breathing exercises.* HOPE *enters as Griselda, with the violin case. At the sight of him, she stops and stands staring at him with adoration*)

CORKLEY (*Rising, after a few seconds*) Uh . . . that's very good, Hope . . . that goofy look as if you're in love with the guy . . . Keep it! But let's have the first line a little sooner.

HOPE (*Snapping out of it, flustered*) Oh! Oh . . . yes . . . I'm sorry . . . (*She goes upstage again, and makes her entrance into the set again, looks at him, then speaks*) Hello, Mr. Prong.

CORKLEY No, no, Miss Springfield! His name in the picture, please . . . It's Kid . . .

HOPE Oh, of course . . . I'm so sorry. (*Once again she goes upstage and makes another entrance. During these attempts,* BYRON's *disdain has been obvious—and once again he begins his punching exercise*) "Hello, Kid."

BYRON (*As Kid*) "Griselda Swann! What are *you* doing here? A famous violinist!"

HOPE (*As Griselda*) "I found out where you were training and I just had to come down."

BYRON "Aaagh . . . I don't know nothin' about that long-haired concerto stuff . . . I'm not an artist . . . I'm just a—pug!"
    (*He tries to hit his palm with his fist; the first time he misses*)

HOPE (*Putting down her violin case and rushing to him*) "Oh, but you *are* an artist . . . Your muscles ripple like the strings of a great instrument!"

(*He grabs her and bends her back in a passionate film embrace. Then he sets her on her feet quickly, pushes her aside, and abruptly walks away.* HOPE *is obviously flustered but thrilled, as she steadies herself*)

BYRON "Aaaaaaagh! We come from different worlds! You don't care nothin' about boxing . . ."

HOPE "Oh, I don't know . . . I lost my voice screaming with everyone else at the St. Nicholas Arena last week . . . when someone in black trunks came out sluggin' in the fourth round and flattened Ritzy Reff . . ."

BYRON "You came to see me fight?"

HOPE (*Moving toward him slowly—arms outstretched*) "I came . . . I saw . . . You conquered!"

CORKLEY Cut! (BYRON *leaves* HOPE *standing there expectantly, as he drops his passionate expression and goes in a business-like fashion to his chair to put on his robe and exit.* CORKLEY *comes to* HOPE) Now, Hope . . . Here is where you play the violin . . .

HOPE I play the violin . . . ?

CORKLEY We'll take care of everything . . . You just supply the emotion! (*Calling offstage*) Okay, boys, bring that backing! (MYRA *comes to help* HOPE *take off her hat and coat. While she does this, two men dressed completely in black—including hoods—enter, one carrying the violin, the other the bow. Except for the fact that they carry these and that each is wearing a long white glove on one arm, they look exactly like medieval executioners. Two stagehands bring on a black backing flat.* HOPE *turns, sees the hooded figures, and screams,* CORKLEY *brings her—unwillingly—to center)* Just put your hands behind your back!

*(*HOPE *does, and at a signal from* CORKLEY, *the four men surround* HOPE—*two of them holding the flat behind her, and the other two standing directly behind her, holding and playing the violin, which has been placed under her chin. As* HOPE *moves about—to the music of Paganini's "Caprice" blaring over the sound system—she is at first astonished at the fingering and fiddling rapidly moving beneath her very eyes . . . then she joins in the game with great gusto . . . the four men moving in step with her about the stage, as she looks passionately fraught. The music ends abruptly, and she finds herself holding the bow and violin in her own hands, the two men having withdrawn theirs. She looks at the fiddle and bow with a delighted giggle)*

Blackout

Scene Six

A spotlight picks out a plump lady commentator, who resembles and sounds like a famous one. She is standing behind a microphone.

DORA DAILEY (*In a singsong, over-sincere manner*) This is Dora Dailey . . . your Voice of Hollywood. Excitement is running high at the F.F.F. Studios! They have a new mystery star who they are keeping under wraps . . . and for the past two weeks Ralph Governor has been forging ahead with *The Fiddler and the Fighter,* in his uncle's absence. L.Z. Governor is still looking for talent in far-off Vienna, that beautiful country which gave us . . . Maurice Chevalier.

Blackout

Scene Seven

Dr. Traurig's office in Vienna. A leather analyst's couch, a small table, and a chair are placed before a large casement window through which a section of the city can be seen. Above the window stands a bust of Sigmund Freud.

DR. ANTON TRAURIG, a small, bearded Viennese gentleman, with pince-nez and in morning clothes, is seated by the table, his notebook in hand. On his couch lies the powerful, portly, be-moustached figure of the great L.Z. GOVERNOR himself, dressed in a pin-striped, double-breasted business suit. He looks troubled and ill at ease.

TRAURIG Mr. Governor . . . please continue . . .

L.Z. (*Springing up impatiently and starting to pace menacingly, like an angry bull*) This is taking too long! I gotta get back to America . . . I gotta get back to my studio—They call me two, three—five times a day! I got my latest discovery out there . . . and six idiot nephews!

TRAURIG You Americans are all in such a hurry! Psychoanalysis takes time, Mr. Governor . . . it takes time! Now lie down! (L.Z. *lies down reluctantly*) Let us return to your recurrent nightmare . . .

L.Z. Well . . . I'm a little boy in my classroom at school. My teacher is marking papers with a live snake . . . she is sitting in her chair, naked . . .

TRAURIG (*Dismissing this airily*) Well, this is not signifi-cant . . . This is your mother. Go on . . .

L.Z. (*Sitting up—outraged*) My mother! The finest woman that ever lived! My mother was *never* naked!

TRAURIG Please, Mr. Governor, I am trying to help you . . .

L.Z. You help me by insulting my mother!? Such filth! You *dirty* man!

TRAURIG (*Firmly*) Please continue with your dream. You are in the classroom, yes?

L.Z. (*Lying back*) Ah, let me see . . . ah, yes—I see six boys with dunce caps in a row—and one is trying to put the dunce cap on *me* . . . and take my seat! Over each dunce is a number . . .

TRAURIG Can you tell me these numbers?

L.Z. Uh . . . one, two, three, five, six . . .

TRAURIG (*Making a note*) Aha!

L.Z. Then I see a lot of quick things all in the classroom. Like—I'm running up the Eiffel Tower. Suddenly it collapses. Then I put a cigar in my mouth. One of the dunces lights it . . . and it melts! I fill a fountain pen, but it won't write . . . I see a picture of George Wash-ington . . . he looks like one of my nephews . . . He is chopping down the cherry tree with a hatchet . . . I

49

scream "No! No! No!" . . . and I wake up in a cold sweat.

(*He ends sitting up on couch, highly agitated*)

TRAURIG   Aha! Now what does all this mean?

L.Z.   It means I had a lousy night's sleep!

TRAURIG   It means you are undergoing extreme anxieties. These are all sex symbols . . .

L.Z. (*Furious*)   Sex! I never think about sex! I'm a married man! You dirty . . . *dirty* man! (*Lies down again, muttering*) Ah, I thought this would take two, three, five days . . . and out!

TRAURIG   Those numbers again!

L.Z.   What numbers?

TRAURIG   I think we are getting somewhere! Let us examine these numbers. Now, at school you must have studied the Gettysburg Address. How does it start?

L.Z.   "Five score and seven years ago . . ."

TRAURIG   Aha! Now, on the golf course when someone is in your way, what do you yell?

L.Z.   "Get outa my way!"

TRAURIG   Aha! (*Rising*) Why can't you say the number "four"—? (L.Z. *sits up suddenly, looking stricken.*

TRAURIG *paces as he expounds*) Since you are a busy man . . . I shall give you a quick answer and let you go. You are at the dangerous age. Your power is centered in your studio and you are afraid that someone is trying to usurp it. The number four terrifies you . . . therefore, this must have something to do with the number four. We must find the connection. We find it by free association . . . Now, say the first thing that comes into your head . . . King.

L.Z. Me.

TRAURIG Aha—slaves.

L.Z. My nephews!

TRAURIG—Aha! Empire.

L.Z. The studio I built—the power that is mine!

TRAURIG Four! (L.Z. *opens his mouth—nothing comes out*) Wunderschön! You're doing fine . . . Julius Caesar.

L.Z. (*Rising*) Me.

TRAURIG Traitors.

L.Z. My nephews.

TRAURIG Four! (L.Z. *opens his mouth and gags.* TRAURIG *sits on the couch beside him*) Wunderschön! It's coming through! Dunce.

51

L.Z. Nephews.

TRAURIG Nephews.

L.Z. Six.

TRAURIG One.

L.Z. Frank.

TRAURIG Two.

L.Z. George.

TRAURIG Three.

L.Z. Harold.

TRAURIG Four.

L.Z. (*With difficulty*) Ralph.

TRAURIG Four!

L.Z. Ralph!

TRAURIG (*Emphatically*) Ralph!

L.Z. (*Jumping up and running about joyously, like a child released from school*) Four! Four! Four! Aha! *Ralph!* He's out to get me—that Arnold Benedict! Thank you, Doctor! Now I can get back to my studio!

TRAURIG   But we have cured only one symptom! Your basic trouble is still your sex anxieties!

L.Z.   Don't say that word—you dirty man!

TRAURIG   I am not a dirty man! I am a scientist!

L.Z.   Then you're a dirty scientist!

Blackout

Scene Eight

On the set, there is much the same bustling activity as before, with dancers energetically rehearsing a number. Pieces of scenery, electrical equipment, and a group of platforms of varying heights are in the background. CORKLEY, *watching the rehearsal from downstage, interrupts it by blowing a whistle.*

CORKLEY Cut! Get Miss Springfield and Mr. Prong! All right, dancers . . . make your change!
> (*The dancers break and exit in several directions as* RALPH *enters with his usual urgency*)

RALPH Custer—I just got a cable from Uncle Lionel. He's on the train! He'll be here in two days . . . I want this picture finished before he gets here . . .

CORKLEY But, Ralph!

RALPH Don't tell me about your ulcer . . . Two days! (HOPE *and* BYRON *enter, in rehearsal clothes*) Hope, the rushes look great. You're great!

HOPE Well, if I am great, it's only because of you . . . and Custer . . . and Byron! I mean—nobody is greater than Byron!

BYRON (*Crossing to the piano*) She's right!

CORKLEY All right, children. Now we'll do the big song
  . . . Let's rehearse it!
      (RALPH *exits.* BYRON *sits down at the upright piano.*
      CORKLEY *hands a piece of music to* HOPE, *then be-*
      gins to move about, checking his camera angles as
      they rehearse)

BYRON (*Sings "I'm With You"*)
  I'm with you—
  You pick the tune, I'll dance it.
  I'm with you—
  You call the shot, I'll chance it.
      (*He rises and leaves the piano, going to* HOPE *at*
      center)
  Lead the way,
  Right or wrong,
  No questions asked—
  I'll string along . . .
      (*Two stagehands enter and stand leaning against*
      the piano as they listen)
  My hopes were gone—
  Then you turned up to choose me.
  From now on—
  You're never gonna lose me.
  I'm with you—
  Yes, I'm with you—
  I won't change partners
  'Cause I'm happy to spend all my time with . . .
  Happy to live on a dime with . . .

Happy to live . . . long as I'm with . . .
You.

(HOPE *and* BYRON *are revolved offstage, and the
equivalent of a movie "dissolve" takes place as we
see the finished number as it will appear on the
screen—in full costume, and in all the black and
white splendor of a musical extravaganza of the
mid-thirties. As the lights dim, the platforms turn
and magically become a grand curved staircase,
down which descend a gorgeous array of lady vio-
linists in enormous picture hats, silvery hair, and
spiraled gossamer gowns. The men accompanying
them are dancers, all attired in white tie and white
tails, who spin about the ladies, Fred Astaire style,
with a million taps to each step. The ladies each
play a violin as they glide about majestically, ethe-
really caroling an "Oo-oo-oo" obligato to the sono-
rous singing and stringing strains of the orchestra's
"I'm With You." A series of arches—outlines of
violins—illuminated by hundreds of glittering
lights descend from above and sail in from the
wings, against a shimmering backdrop of lights. A
dozen girl-violins dance on, all be-stringed from
necklines to navels . . . their male partners happily
plucking these strings as they all tap up and down
the stairs.*

*Against a blaze of lights sparkling on the set, cos-
tumes, and instruments, tall showgirls enter,
scantily clad—as harp, lute, banjos, and a grand
piano. At one point the stage is completely darkened
and we can see only the instruments aglow as they
seem to float through a series of geometric forma-*

tions that strongly suggests the famous Busby Berk-
ley overhead shots. For a finale HOPE *and* BYRON
re-enter; she is dressed in a dazzling Cinderella-like
gown and a silver crown, BYRON *in a silver boxing*
outfit, complete with silver boxing gloves. Once
more they sing, while the entire ensemble keep
happily whirling away toward the celestially thrill-
ing conclusion)

HOPE *and* BYRON
 I'm with you—
 Yes, I'm with you—
 I won't change partners
 'Cause I'm happy to spend all my time with—
 Happy to live on a dime with—

ALL
 Happy to live . . . long as I'm . . . with . . . you . . .
 You!
 (This majestic tableau is suddenly interrupted by
 the entrance of CORKLEY, *blowing his whistle and*
 shouting)

CORKLEY Save your lights! Save 'em!

RALPH *(Entering with* RUDOLF *and the other nephews)*
That's it! That wraps it up!

CORKLEY Strike the set! Move down here, everybody—
Mr. Ralph has something to say to you. Let's have that
backing!
 (At CORKLEY's *directions, the company break from*
 their positions and move out of the elaborate set to

57

group themselves around the executives. At the same time, the scenery is wafted out of sight, staircases revolve, stagehands shift equipment, and a colorful backdrop descends behind the actors, masking the movie set)

RALPH *(Excited and in charge)* Ladies and gentlemen . . . We brought it in in three weeks! *(The group applaud)* Thank you—thank you! And we did it just in time, kiddies. L.Z. Governor gets here early tomorrow morning. Hope—I'm so proud of you . . .

HOPE Thank you, Mr. Ralph . . .

RALPH *(Expansively)* So darned proud. And a month from now they'll be applauding you in movie theatres all over the country . . . *Now*, Don . . .

LEAD DANCER *(Stepping forward to HOPE)* Hope, the kids on the set all got together and chipped in to give you this silver flashlight!
(He presents her with a be-jeweled flashlight, tied with a large bow)

HOPE *(Taking it)* Oh, thanks! I sure wish I'd had this when I was an usherette! And I especially want to thank my mother . . . for her complete lack of faith in me. If it hadn't been for her constant discouragement, I wouldn't be here today!

BYRON *(Trying desperately to be included)* And as your co-star . . .

RALPH And for everyone's hard work, I am giving you all
a little party—champagne and cake on Stage Twelve.
Change your costumes!
(*The group begin to break up and exit, chattering
happily*)

BYRON And as your co-star . . .

RALPH (*To* HOPE) And I have a surprise for you! I've
got something terrific lined up for you next!
(*He whispers very confidentially into her ear*)

HOPE (*Overjoyed*) You mean I'm going to dance with
Fred Astaire? (BYRON *hasn't missed any of this by-play;
he stamps off in a rage*) Byron, wait! I'll give you a lift
down to Stage Twelve!
(RALPH *exits as* HOPE *starts after* BYRON, *but she
bumps into* RUDOLF, *who has planted himself in
her path*)

RUDOLF (*Tentatively*) Hope? (*She stares at him im-
patiently as he unfolds a piece of paper*) Uh . . . you
see what I wrote on this? It's what I once said to you:
"This girl is not the movie type." (*He chuckles*) Well,
I'm ready to eat my words . . .
(*He starts to put the paper in his mouth*)

HOPE Thanks, Randolph . . .
(*She exits hastily, having barely listened to him*)

RUDOLF (*Cringing, as from a blow*) Randolph?
(*Sings "Notice Me"*)

59

You didn't even know my name.
You didn't even see my face.
You stared at me so blankly,
Like staring into space.
I'm not a piece of furniture,
A hat rack . . . or a brass spittoon.
I've got to change,
I've got to change . . .

I've got to make you notice me,
Make you smile at me,
Make you know I'm alive.
Got to make your eyes light up,
Make your arms reach out
When you see me arrive.
Got to find the way,
Learn the things to say,
So one day you don't look through me,
You'll run right to me . . .
I die . . . when I see you look at him,
See you smile at him,
See you run at his call.
Wonder what you see in him,
What you want with him,
Why you want him at all . . .
Starting now here's how it's gonna be—
I'll move right in for the kill,
Overpower your will . . .
Till you take notice of no one but me!
    (*He exits determinedly as the lights fade*)

Scene Nine

The executive dining room. As before, six chairs and "the throne" are placed around a long table, on which there is now a telephone.

BYRON (*Entering and pacing angrily, alone until* RALPH *enters*) Ralph, I've got to see L.Z.! What's this rotten rumor that Fred Astaire is gonna be playing opposite Hope Springfield in her next picture, instead of *me*? Is that fair?!

RALPH Cool off, Byron . . . (*He picks up the receiver and speaks into the phone*) We'll show the picture in here. (*Putting it down*) L.Z. just got off the train two hours ago . . . he's tired . . . he's having his massage, and then we're running the picture for him. We're all much too busy for your petty little problems . . .

BYRON (*Enraged*) Petty! I tell you, L.Z. won't let you do this to me! I'll be in that next picture with Hope Springfield, in spite of what you say! I made this studio what it is today! They should be using my face for the trademark, instead of that crummy seal's!

RALPH (*On his way out*) Have you taken a look at it lately?
(*He exits*)

BYRON Lately? It's my only joy in life! (*He takes a mirror from the pocket of his dressing gown and gazes, enraptured, into it*) It's perfect!

> (*And he sings a love song, "My Fortune Is My Face," to himself. The melody is a very French waltz—languorously self-indulgent*)
> My fortune is my face—
> Laughing . . . crying . . . smiling . . .
> Look upon this face—
> Wistful . . . scornful . . . and beguiling.
> Right profile . . . left profile . . .
> Three quarters . . . and full face—
> Perfect!
> Every angle right—cameraman's delight.
> Thirty-two dazzling teeth—a sight divine!
> Thirty-two . . . one of them is nearly mine.
> My fortune is my face—
> Manly . . . boyish . . . leering . . .
> All this in one face—
> Eager . . . evil . . . and endearing.
> Right profile! Left profile!
> A face unique from any view.
> When this face is gone, gone is fortune, too!
> (*He speaks into the mirror*)

All right, face . . . Keep it up . . . Keep working! There's a lot depending on you—whole gambling syndicate. Can't keep it going without you! Three ex-wives . . . all that alimony . . . and six kids!! And all *their* teeth to be fixed! Teeth! Stretching for miles and miles into the horizon . . . !

(*Sings*)
Right profile! Left profile!
Three quarters . . . and full face!
So pin it up with tacks . . .
And fill it out with wax . . .
　　(*Laughs*)
Oh, what an actor!
Long live Max Factor!
And . . . this . . . face!
　　(*He hastily pockets his mirror as* RALPH, RUDOLF
　　*and the other nephews enter and go to their
　　chairs*)

RALPH　They're pleased I went ahead on my own . . .
Very pleased . . .
　　(*The phone rings.* RUDOLF *picks it up*)

RUDOLF　Yes?

RALPH　The Board of Directors in New York realizes that
a studio shouldn't be run by one man alone . . .

RUDOLF　Uncle Lionel has finished his massage . . .
　　(*He puts the phone down*)

BYRON　I want to talk to him!

RUDOLF　He'll be right in.

RALPH　I'm not saying Uncle Lionel isn't great . . . but
he's old—old and great . . . and I'm young—young and
great. And we've got here a great little picture and a

great new star! This may be the beginning of a new era out here at F.F.F.!
(L.Z. *enters in a terry robe, smoking a cigar*)

BYRON (*Heartily*) Hi, L.Z.! Welcome back! I want to talk to you—

L.Z. Not now, Byron. Tomorrow. (*He goes to sit on his throne. To* RUDOLF) Get me the bungalow.

RUDOLF Yessir.
(*Picks up the phone and dials*)

BYRON Listen, L.Z., wait'll you see this picture! Springfield and I are the greatest team ever . . . And in our next picture together—I—

L.Z. (*Cutting him off*) Who said you're gonna be in it? How do you know she wants you? If she's what they tell me she is . . . we may get her Gable, Astaire. Anybody she wants!

BYRON (*Turning pale*) I think she'll want *me*!
(*He turns and exits through the door*)

L.Z. So . . . you did it all by yourself, my Nephew Number *Four*!
(*He laughs to himself, replaces his cigar in his mouth*)

RALPH (*Sitting to* L.Z.'s *left*) Uncle Lionel, the girl's great!

64

L.Z.   I know the girl's great. My guts don't lie!

RALPH   Only—ha, ha—Rudolf here . . . said she wasn't your type.

ARNOLD (*Chuckling*)   That's what he said!

L.Z. (*Menacing*)   You did, Rudolf?

RUDOLF (*Holding the phone*)   Well, yes . . . but, after all, what do *I* know?

L.Z.   "What do I know?" (*He guffaws*) Idiot!

RUDOLF (*Into the phone*)   Hope . . . It's Uncle Lionel . . .
    (*He hands the phone to* L.Z.)

L.Z. (*His manner and tone change to sweetness*)   Welcome to F.F.F.! My dear, I will send a car around for you at seven . . . and take you and show you off to the world, at the Coconut Grove. Oh, and I have been brooding over your name . . . Hope Springfield . . . a delicious name, but not for merchandising. So tonight I have an engagement with my great new star . . . "Lila Tremaine" . . . How do you like it? (*Covers phone, speaking to the nephews*) She loves it! (*Back into the phone*) See you later . . . Lila Tremaine! Goodbye. (*He hangs up. Back to his rough tone*) All right! Run the film!
    (RUDOLF *signals, and the lights dim on the stage as the beam from a projector machine glitters from an opening in center wall, above the portrait. The*

65

men face front as though watching a screen; there is dim light on the faces watching. We hear the sound track of the film . . . and, later, simultaneous dialogue on stage)

UNCTUOUS MALE VOICE Kid . . . before you leave the settlement house, I'd like you to meet a very special young lady—Griselda Swann.

KID'S VOICE Sorry, Father McGruder—I've got to run . . . big fight tonight at the St. Nicholas Arena, and I— did you say Griselda Swann?

GRISELDA'S VOICE Hello, Kid . . .

KID'S VOICE Griselda Swann . . . you were just a skinny kid with braces when I saw you last . . .

L.Z. Who's that?

RALPH (*Chuckling at the joke*) Ha ha . . . "Who's that?"

GRISELDA'S VOICE Kid . . . I never knew you noticed me. I dreamed of you every night after that for nearly a year.

L.Z. Skip to her entrance . . .

RALPH Whose entrance?

KID'S VOICE Gee.

L.Z. My girl's. Hope Springfield—

GRISELDA'S VOICE You were my Ragamuffin Prince Charming . . . with the fists of a bully, but the

RALPH That's her! Isn't she great?

L.Z. Who?

66

eyes of a poet! The girls in the neighborhood all adored you. Me—I just wasn't in the running. I knew it. You seemed so —unattainable! I tried to put you out of my mind, but you came back to haunt me—every night, all night long!

KID'S VOICE Gee—every night? Say . . . (*Chuckle, chuckle*) did I ever give you a tumble in your dreams?

GRISELDA'S VOICE Never . . . never . . . you were always running away— running, running . . . A two-fisted will-o'-the-wisp! And your eyes seemed to taunt me and say . . . "Silly girl with braces— not you—silly, silly girl!"

KID'S VOICE Gee . . .

RALPH Hope Springfield.

L.Z. Where is she?

RALPH There she is—just be patient . . . you'll see plenty of her. There's an hour and a half of film!

L.Z. (Pointing at the screen) Of *her*??

RALPH Well, who else?

L.Z. (*Annoyed*) Where's Hope Springfield?

RALPH (*Laughing*) Welllll . . . the one in the boxing trunks is Byron Prong. So the other one . . . is Hope Springfield! Your personal discovery!

L.Z. (*Screams*) Stop that film! Turn on the lights! (*The lights have come back up in the room; the sound track is silent*) You've done a great job, Ralph, and you did it

67

all without me! You made only one little mistake. *She's the wrong girl!* (*Jumps up, threatening* RALPH. RALPH *gets up, as do all the other nephews*) Burn that film—the whole thing!

RALPH (*As* L.Z. *pursues him*)   But . . . but . . . you picked her from the line—you told me—

L.Z.   Sure, I picked her from the line . . . One, two, three . . . five . . . Five! Aha! I said five instead of four—it was all *your* fault! My fine Nephew Number Four! (*Shaking his finger at* RALPH) You made me sick in my head. But now I'm cured! My ambitious Nephew Number Four—you're fired!

NEPHEWS (*Quickly*)   It was all him, Uncle Lionel . . . We had nothing to do with it . . . We knew something was wrong . . .

L.Z.   But who amongst you tried to stop him? Not a one—but *you,* my boy . . . (*Turning to* RUDOLF) My favorite nephew . . .

RUDOLF (*Backing away*)   No . . . no . . .

L.Z.   You—you, my brilliant boy . . . who wasn't afraid to say the emperor had no clothes on . . . for this I make you vice-president in charge of production!

RUDOLF   No! Uncle Lionel . . . you can't! I'm stupid!

L.Z.   That's what I like!
          (*He takes* RUDOLF *by the arm*)

68

RUDOLF   But I'm spineless!

L.Z.   I will personally call New York and get the right
girl out here immediately . . . the right Number Four
. . . and start the picture over. As for that other girl,
Hope Springfield, I'll have her thrown off the lot at
once!

RUDOLF (*Stricken*)   Oh, Uncle Lionel . . . that poor girl!

L.Z.   I don't want anybody around this town that reminds
me of my mistakes! Get her out!

RUDOLF   You can't! I mean—you're such an important
figure . . . a giant . . . head of one of the biggest movie
studios in the world. You can't be so brutal!

L.Z.   You're right. *You* do it!
      (*He exits*)

RUDOLF (*Crushed; ironically*)   Now she'll notice me.
      (*Sings*)
   We're the oldest union out here . . .

NEPHEWS
   The oldest union out here . . .

ALL
   The brotherhood of *Fear*!

(*The lights fade*)

Scene Ten

The bungalow. What we see of it is an overdecorated sitting room, with several doors leading to other rooms. At center is a large window draped with fluffy white curtains, flanked by two overflowing flower stands and displaying a white cupid statue placed at the center of the window. The walls are a shade of lavender, and the reigning motif is a heart design—decorating the silken door frames and window trim—like a bad-taste Valentine. The furnishings are predominantly white: a large, deep-cushion couch; near it, a low coffee table on which is a gold and white telephone, and a huge pouffe. DORA DAILEY, seated on the couch with pad and pencil, is interviewing HOPE, who at the moment is showing her a gold evening gown.

DORA How lovely!

HOPE And tonight Mr. Governor is taking me to the Coconut Grove! Oh, and just a few minutes ago Mr. Governor telephoned me. That's when I found out they had changed my name to Lila Tremaine!

DORA I'll announce your new name on my program next Sunday . . . Lulu.

HOPE Lila . . .

DORA (Rising, preparing to leave) Bless you! I'm your friend . . . and anything that happens concerning ro-

mance or career . . . just you telephone silly old Dora—
first! Or your name will be mud in this town!

HOPE   Oh, Dora!
    (*They hug each other*)

DORA   Goodbye . . . Lilly Ptomaine . . .
    (*She exits*)

HOPE   (*Calling after her*)   Lila Tremaine! (*To herself*)
Lila Tremaine . . . (*She sits on the pouffe. She is in a
robe, a scarf on her head to cover the curlers in her hair.
There is a knock on the door*) Come in! (BYRON *enters,
carrying a bottle of champagne in a bucket, and two
champagne glasses*) Byron!

BYRON   Hello, you!

HOPE   (*Wildly taking the curlers out of her hair, removing
her scarf*)   Byron! Why didn't you call? I must look a
mess!

BYRON   You look ravishing! A little celebration for the
end of our first picture together.
    (*He opens the bottle*)

HOPE   (*Totally overwhelmed*)   Oh, Byron—what a surprise!
    (*She is flustered, finishing her hair*)

BYRON   I thought I'd just sneak over while L.Z. is running
your film . . . and grab a moment with you . . .
    (*He pours the champagne*)

HOPE   But, Byron. You've hardly spoken to me since we
met . . . and suddenly here you are in my bungalow!

BYRON I know . . . blind fool that I've been! We've wasted so much time, Hope . . .

HOPE We have?

BYRON (*Hands her a glass*) Let's drink to the new power at the studio—you! My co-star! Hope Springfield!
(*They drink*)

HOPE Oh—haven't you heard? They changed my name . . . It's Lila Tremaine!

BYRON (*Stares at her a moment*) Lila Tremaine . . . it suits you. Do you feel different?

HOPE Oh, yes! Did you feel different?

BYRON When?

HOPE When they changed your name from Harry Doppelfinger?

BYRON (*Taken aback but covering up, he grins and laughs across at her.* HOPE *grins and laughs back*) You know everything, don't you? (HOPE *affects a nonchalant gesture with her right hand, forgets she is holding a glass, and spills champagne on the floor*) Let's drink to a series of co-starring films together until they invent a new word for . . . love-making! (HOPE *gulps down remainder of her champagne, and with a delicately arched finger, puts the last drops of her champagne like perfume behind her ears.* BYRON *sits next to her, on the pouffe*) You know . . . I've been watching you . . . *feeling* you. You're a budding new star—but I've had such great experience. I could teach you so much.

HOPE (*Turning to him*)   When does school start?

BYRON   Now.
　　(*He takes her in his arms, kisses her*)

HOPE   Can we skip a grade?
　　(*They indulge in a series of quick kisses, nose to nose*)

BYRON   You know, you don't sing nearly enough in this picture . . . There's a moment lacking—the Prong-Tremaine moment! The big song . . . (*Sings*)
　　My heart is like—

HOPE (*Sings, picking it up from him*)
　　A violin . . . the tune comes out when you come in . . .

BYRON   You know the song!

HOPE   Know it? I've been listening to you singing it in your dressing room for three weeks! Oh, I just love it!

BYRON (*Cheek to cheek*)   My darling, that song must be in the picture!
　　(*He turns her to him, kisses her; they hum the song while kissing*)

HOPE (*Breaking the kiss*)   Byron, you're right! (*Hypnotized—she rises*) That song has *got* to be in the picture! I'll tell Lionel Z. Governor himself tonight!

BYRON   Good girl!

HOPE (*Ecstatic*)   Oh, Byron—just think! Soon we'll be dancing and singing our way into the hearts of America —together!

(*He rises and they do a mad Astaire-Rogers-type dance together, while they sing the melody of "My Heart Is Like a Violin." They end in a passionate, bent-over embrace, near the couch. The phone rings*)

HOPE (*Still bent over, she reaches back and picks it up*) Hello? (BYRON *is running wild kisses over her neck, shoulders, arms*) Byron Prong? I'll see if he's here. (*She hands the phone to him—he kisses her wrist and hand before taking phone*) It's your agent.

    (BYRON *sets her upright and sits on the end of the couch to talk into the phone.* HOPE *staggers to the pouffe and gingerly eases down on it—she is dizzy and her back is strained from the long embrace*)

BYRON (*Into the phone*) Lyman? What are you calling me *here* for? What? When did *that* happen? (*He looks suddenly at* HOPE, *with an altogether changed expression*) Are you sure? All right. Thanks, old boy. (*He hangs up, pours the champagne from his glass back into the champagne bottle*) I've got to go . . .

    (*He rises, taking the champagne bottle with him, and starts for the door*)

HOPE (*Rising—surprised*) Oh, Byron . . . I'm sorry.

BYRON (*Moving toward the door*) Yeah, yeah . . . it's tough . . . but I've gotta leave.

HOPE You look so strange! Is anything wrong?

BYRON No—no! Well, see you around . . .

HOPE In school—tomorrow?

74

BYRON   Oh, yeah . . . school. Listen, if I'm not here . . .
you start without me. Goodbye—*Lila* . . .
        (*He exits.* HOPE *stands there, happily transfixed as
        she hears the magical name, and starts repeating it
        to herself, hypnotically*)

HOPE   Lila Tremaine . . . Lila Tremaine . . . Lila Tremaine! (*Slouching*) Hope Springfield . . . (*Changing to
a chesty pose*) Lila Tremaine! (*She cackles like a witch*)
Goodbye, Hope Springfield—you've had it! (*She pre-
tends to stir a witch's brew, then holds a vial of it in her
hand*) From now on, you're . . .
        (*To a sinister musical accompaniment, she drinks
        down the draught, and instantly transforms herself
        into a femme fatale as she sings an ecstatic little
        refrain of "A Girl to Remember"—very operatic—
        half chesty contralto, and half coloratura*)

Lila Tremaine, Lila Tremaine . . .
Li-la, Li-la, Li-la, Li-la—Tremaine!
Lila Tremaine, Lila Tremaine . . .
Li-la, Li-la, Li-la, Li-la—Tremaine!
        (*Then, with great jazzy energy*)

Roll out the carpet, fetch my car!
Fade out—fade in . . . today I'm a star!

I'm gonna be, gonna be a name—
A name to remember—
Neon they'll see on a sign!
They're gonna see something rarer
Than a rose in December—
They'll send me mail, wait in line!
What I think, what I say

Will be headlines every day!
What I drink, lipstick I use
Will be in the news—over and over!
I'll make the crowd
Shout out loud when I come out—
There she is!
It's me!
A name to remember—
Me!
A girl to remember—
Me!
That's what I'm gonna be!

Millions of people will applaud
When I get my Academy Award!

I'm gonna make
Every brake in traffic stop—
There she is!
It's me!
A face to remember—
Me!
A girl to remember—
Me!
That's who I'm gonna be!

(*During the last notes of her song,* RUDOLF *enters with a hangdog expression . . . and watches as* HOPE, *unaware of his presence, jumps onto the pouffe, clutching an imaginary Oscar. He stands there for a moment, hand on his brow—then starts walking toward her as the music swells and* HOPE *happily begins to blow kisses to her millions of invisible admirers*)
                              Curtain

Act Two

Scene One

DORA DAILEY'S *voice is heard over an offstage micro-phone.*

DORA Excitement is running high at the F.F.F. Studios over the arrival of gorgeous Gloria Currie—the *real* Lila Tremaine—who will star in the new version of *The Fiddler and the Fighter.* The entire old version, starring Hope Springfield, the *false* Lila Tremaine, had to be scrapped . . . but L.Z. Governor resumed production with the minimum of repercussions. "We all make mistakes," he said . . . and fired 736 people!

Scene Two

The wardrobe department. MYRA *and the seamstress are putting last-minute touches on a costume worn by an actress.*

VESPERS (*Enters, calling*) They're ready for you, Betty!
    (*The actress glides out, followed by* VESPERS . . . *as* RUDOLF *enters from the opposite direction, carrying a suitcase from which a shirt sleeve protrudes*)

RUDOLF (*Nervously*) Myra!

MYRA (*As she sends the seamstress offstage with some costumes*) Oh, hello, Mr. Rudolf . . .

RUDOLF Can I leave this here till tonight?

MYRA (*As he places the suitcase under the table*) Oh, sure, sure . . . Planning a quick getaway after the first day of shooting? What's in there?

RUDOLF Oh, just some old clothes . . .

MYRA You did a beautiful job of packing!
    (*She picks up the bag and places it on the table, opening it and preparing to repack it*)

RUDOLF (*Going quickly to her, trying to stop her*) No! No, don't bother to . . .

(MYRA *has already picked up and held out to him two cans of film*)

MYRA   Large cuff links.
(*She looks at him questioningly*)

RUDOLF (*Whispering. Very nervous*)   It's all the film there is on Hope. I didn't burn it. I stole it. I'm taking it home.

MYRA (*Replacing the cans of film, folding the shirt inside, closing and replacing the suitcase under the table*) Where is Hope?

RUDOLF   I can't find her.
(*They are interrupted by a* BOY *wheeling in a small rolling platform on which there is an enormous, tall floral arrangement*)

BOY   Flowers for Miss Lila Tremaine!

MYRA (*To* RUDOLF, *as she goes toward the screen*)   She can wear *that* on her shoulder strap! (*Calling inside*) Miss Tremaine! Ready? There's something here for you!
(GLORIA CURRIE *enters, in a low-cut, sexy, bare midriff—looking devastating. She has the icy beauty of a showgirl type, and is very sure of herself. She is also very stupid*)

GLORIA (*Seeing the flowers*)   For me? Ohh! (*She squeals —then hurries to the flowers and reads the card attached*) "A few posies for your first day of shooting . . ."

(*From the back of the huge bouquet, two hands push the flowers aside and the head of* L.Z. GOV-ERNOR *pops out*)

L.Z. *Surprise!!!* (GLORIA *gasps with pleasure*) Now close your eyes and put out your arm . . . (*Looking roguish, he puts a diamond bracelet on her*) Surprise!

GLORIA (*Opening her eyes wide*) Ohhh, Mr. Governor! I don't know what to say!
  (L.Z. *comes out from behind the flowers and calls outside*)

L.Z. All right—everybody in! (*The nephews, except for* RALPH, *enter with* ROSCOE *and all the technical staff.* BOY *pushes floral piece off. Indicating* GLORIA) Isn't that something! Look at that! (*Beside himself*) That's *what I call a fiddler!* (*He turns to* GLORIA, *takes her hand*) Well, Lila Tremaine . . . this is the beginning of a great career! And how do we feel this morning?
  (L.Z. *pinches her cheek . . . he cannot take eyes or hands off her*)

GLORIA Oh, just swell, Uncle Lionel!

L.Z. (*To the others*) "Uncle Lionel" . . . isn't that sweet? (*Calls across to* RUDOLF) Rudolf, you're a lucky boy! The first picture you direct and you have *this*! (*He indicates* GLORIA) You ready to shoot?

RUDOLF We've been working on the scene where she first meets the Kid—

L.Z. Good. Let's hear it.

GLORIA   Oh, oh, yes—at the settlement house. I looked it over.

RUDOLF   (*Going to* GLORIA, *showing her the script*)   Uh . . . right here on page twelve . . . The Kid says . . . "Griselda Swann. You were just a skinny kid with braces when I saw you last—" (*Pause; then he repeats the cue*) ". . . skinny kid with braces when I saw you last—"

GLORIA   (*Hastily taking the script*)   Oh, well—perhaps I'd better read it, to be sure. (*She giggles at* L.Z., *who giggles back. In a monotone*) "Kid, I never knew you noticed me—I dreamed of you every night after that for yearly a near."

RUDOLF   Excuse me, Miss Tremaine . . . the line—it's "I dreamed of you every night after that for *n*early a *y*ear."

GLORIA   That's what I said. "I dreamed of you every night after that for yearly a near."

RUDOLF   "Nearly a year."

GLORIA   "Yearly a near."

RUDOLF   (*Very firmly*)   "Nearly a year."

L.Z.   (*Exploding*)   Idiot! You don't know how to direct! Let *me* read it . . . (*He grabs the script from* RUDOLF, *and bellows dramatically*) "I dreamed of you every night after that for *yearly* a *near!*" (*A pause, then, covering up for himself—to* GLORIA) When you're doing it with Byron Prong instead of that soup chicken, you'll have no trouble at all!

GLORIA (*Petulantly*) But, Uncle Lionel . . . I haven't re-hearsed with Byron Prong yet—I haven't even met him!

L.Z. (*Enraged*) Why not?

RUDOLF You put him in another picture.

L.Z. Well, we had two weeks—I couldn't have him laying around doing nothing! (*To* RUDOLF) Get him up here right away!

RUDOLF Yessir!
(*He runs out*)

L.Z. And while we wait, let's have some pictures of this lovely creature!

ROSCOE We gave her some of the same poses as Hope Springfield, and I tell you . . .

GLORIA (*Exploding*) Hope—Hope—Hope! That's all I hear a million times a day! And what did that picture look like? You had to burn it! Listen, back in New York all of us girls knew all along there was a mix-up . . . but, my God, who would have picked her in the first place? And I hear she's still here, working as a manicurist . . .

L.Z. (*Soothingly*) Don't worry about her—she's out! I found her waiting on tables at the Brown Derby . . . I

84

called the manager . . . I said "Out! Out!" Don't you worry about a thing, baby.

GLORIA (*Brightly*) Thanks, Uncle Lionel!
(*She exits behind a screen, followed by* MYRA)

L.Z. Isn't she cute?
(BYRON *storms in, like a mad bull.* BYRON *is wearing the Don Juan outfit—black tights, flowing white shirt, sword and scabbard, Barrymoresque wig, make-up and a penciled moustache. In addition, he is chained into a portable pillory—his head and hands fitted through the holes. He is beside himself with fury*)

BYRON (*Bellowing*) What the hell is this?

L.Z. What's the idea of not rehearsing with my new star —Lila Tremaine!

BYRON (*Pacing, becoming angrier as he speaks*) You put me in this costume quickie—*Don Juan's First Date!* I'm on the set every morning at six . . . I am flogged, hung, thrown into a tank of crocodiles—and on top of that you expect me to rehearse with your latest bagel for a picture I've already made once—(*Rushing at* L.Z.) Lemme out of this thing—I'll kill him!
(*Two nephews step forward and restrain him*)

L.Z. (*To* FRANK) Get me the Don Juan set . . . (*To* BYRON, *as* FRANK *speaks into a phone*) Easy, boy, easy . . . And take this thing off him . . .

85

(Two or three nephews unlatch the pillory. When BYRON *is free, he paces slowly about)*

FRANK *(Handing the phone to* L.Z.*)* Stage Twenty-eight, Uncle Lionel . . .

L.Z. *(Grabbing the phone)* Hello, Matthews . . . I got Prong here. I need him! So finish the picture—now—without him. So he *won't* rescue the girl . . . He's killed by a bolt of lightning. That's right . . . There's no clinch at the end—they don't kiss . . . Instead a close-up of her kissing his picture . . . Fade out. The End . . . What do you mean it's not satisfying? *I'm* satisfied! Look, it's booked into seven hundred theatres already—The public will like it whether they like it or not!
(He hangs up)

FRANK *(Admiringly)* That's picture-making!

L.Z. Byron—I may have just won you your first Academy Award! You die at the end of the picture—that makes you a great actor!

BYRON I'm still not doing the picture with any of your new starlets—!

L.Z. *(Strongly)* You'll start working with your new leading lady today—you'll work every day—and from now on!

BYRON *(Drawing the prop sword he wears)* Never!
*(*L.Z. *jumps back . . . and at this moment* GLORIA

86

comes in again from behind the screen . . . and
BYRON *stands transfixed in his pose)*

GLORIA *(She has mastered it)* "I dreamed of you every
night after that for nearly a year!"

L.Z. *(Beaming at her)* "Nearly a year"—Isn't she cute?
(All applaud, except BYRON. BYRON *and* GLORIA *look at
each other—she has made an instant impact on him.
Severely, to* BYRON*)* Byron—this is Lila Tremaine.
Shake hands.

BYRON *(Going slowly toward her; acting as if he is capitu-
lating reluctantly)* O.K., L.Z., you win! You're a hard
man! How do you do, Miss Tremaine.
*(He kisses her hand and executes a Don Juan bow,
with a flourish)*

GLORIA *(Staring at him)* B.P.—in the flesh!

L.Z. *(Vaguely puzzled)* "B.P.?" What's that "B.P."?

GLORIA It's a game . . . movie stars' initials . . . You have
to guess . . . Like—"J.C."—Jimmy Cagney. "B.P."—
Byron Prong!

L.Z. *(To the nephews)* Isn't that cute?

GLORIA *(Looking at* BYRON's *outfit)* But, Mr. Prong . . .
I thought you were supposed to play a fighter in this! I
never saw boxing trunks like that!! Wow!

L.Z. *(Chuckling)* My dear, those aren't boxing trunks—
they're tights.

87

GLORIA (*Admiringly*) I'll say!

L.Z. Byron . . . you're a good boy. I knew you'd see it my way.

BYRON Sorry I went to pieces, L.Z. All those swashbuckling pictures . . . I guess it's just—battle fatigue.
(*He sings, to an insinuating little South American chanson, "Close Harmony"*)

I'm sorry I blew.
I look up to you.
When talent is picked,
You pick the cream.
I'll do what you say—
I'll slave every day!
Put talent together . . .
You get a great team!

L.Z. *and* BYRON
Close harmony . . . close harmony—
Let's learn from the song birds.
Close harmony . . . close harmony—
Sing-a-ling-ing along,
Harmonizing a song.
(*In the song-and-dance action that follows,* L.Z. *benevolently brings* BYRON *and* GLORIA *into physical contact, which is exactly what they want. As they sing the words of friendship, their insinuating moments of togetherness make it quite plain that their friendship is going much further than* L.Z. *suspects*)

BYRON

So bury the hatchet and saber . . .

L.Z.

Capital should lie down with labor . . .

GLORIA

This even a baby understands!

BYRON

The lion should lie down with the lamb . . .

L.Z.

The oyster should lie down with the clam . . .

GLORIA

Let's take their example—We ought to . . .

L.Z.

Shake hands!

ALL

Close harmony . . . close harmony
Makes friends out of strangers.
Very close harmony . . .
Extra close harmony . . .
Sing along for a change—
"Home on the Range."

GLORIA

Let's find the right key
For you and for me.
We'll do a duet,

For friendship's sake.
We'll do it in thirds—
We'll do without words . . .
And beautiful music
Together we'll make!

ALL

Close harmony . . . close harmony—

GLORIA, BYRON *and* L.Z. (*Barbershop*)
"Tenting on the old camp ground . . ."

ALL

Close harmony . . . close harmony—
Take a tip from the birdies.
Closer and closer and closer . . .
Close harmony!

BYRON (*Speaking to* GLORIA, *as he and* L.Z. *dance around her*) My place tonight?

ALL

Close harmony!

GLORIA (*Speaking to* BYRON) No—mine!

ALL

Close Harmony!
Blackout

A typical Hollywood street . . . actually, a shabby collection of miscellaneous shop windows. The passers-by are a motley group of people. The entire effect of the people and the scene suggests the about-to-be-closed feeling of the unemployed mid-thirties. In the background, however, can be seen the domed top and sign of the glamorous Brown Derby.

HOPE *enters and crosses the stage. She is dressed up in a grotesque Shirley Temple outfit, with a full head of bobbing blond curls, a bow or two, a starched short dress over many petticoats, white socks, and flat Mary Jane shoes. She is also wearing a sandwich sign which bears the legend* KIDDIE KAREER SCHOOL *on front and back. She carries a bunch of blotters which she is trying to give out as she walks along. No one is taking any.*

HOPE (*In a miserably cute little-girl's voice*) Have you a Shirley Temple in your home? Send her to Madame Barrymore's. Turn your little one into a headliner . . . a breadwinner . . . a star! (*Several people pass by*) Have *you* got a Shirley Temple in your home? Send her to Madame Barrymore's . . . Have you got a cunning little cutie at home who can sing and dance and make Mummy and Daddy rich and famous? Hmmm? It's not too early to have another Shirley! Send your kiddy to Madame Barrymore's Kiddie Kareer School . . . (*A woman walking by accepts a blotter*) Thank you, lady!

Baby takes a bow! (HOPE *does a small curtsy*) Bless
Mummy and Daddy . . . and the lady who took the
blotter!

> (LOU WILLIAMS *enters, dressed in a bilious-looking
> green suit, a green derby, pink shirt and tie, yellow
> gloves and spats. He is also wearing a sandwich
> sign, which reads:* MADAME BARRYMORE'S
> DANCING SCHOOL—HOLLYWOOD'S
> TEMPLE OF TERPSICHORE. *He, too, is try-
> ing to pass out blotters*)

LOU   Come to Madame Barrymore's . . . the Queen of
Terpsichore! Tap-tap-tap your way to movie fame. Actors are a dime a dozen . . . Today you gotta dance and
sing. Take one, sir?

> (HOPE *and* LOU *pass each other at this point*)

HOPE (*Wearily*)   Hi, Lou . . .

LOU   How ya doin', Hope?

HOPE (*Groans*)   Agh!

LOU (*Continuing his spiel*)   Learn to dance at Madame
Barrymore's . . . Take one, sir?

> (*Two men pass by without taking a blotter.* HOPE
> *and* LOU *take positions next to each other*)

HOPE   Making any studio rounds, Lou?

LOU (*Shaking his head*)   No one's doing a Civil War
epic.

HOPE Well, I'm not in front of a camera, but at least I *am* in a costume! Last month I was a waitress at the Brown Derby . . . guess who came in and had me fired? L.Z. Governor. Then I tried a job as a manicurist. Guess who came in to have his nails buffed? (*She nods*) "Out! Out!"

LOU (*To a passer-by*) Take one, sir? Come to Madame Barrymore's . . . (*He does a little tap step, but the man goes by. To* HOPE) Nothing since?

HOPE Then I was an usher at the RKO Pantages . . . There I was, up in the second balcony . . . right back where I started—at the bottom!

LOU Things can always get worse . . . Shirley!

HOPE Yes, they can . . . Bojangles! (LOU *bows to her and does a tap step;* HOPE *speaks in a Shirley Temple voice*) So you should be glad, glad, glad!
    (*Sings "You Mustn't Be Discouraged"*)

> When you think you've hit the bottom
> And you're feeling really low,
> You mustn't be discouraged—
> There's always one step further down you can go!
> When you're lying in the gutter,
> Feeling just a bit unsure,
> Just wait until tomorrow—
> You may be lying flat face-down in a sewer!
> Don't be afraid of a little raindrop . . .
> That don't mean nothing, bud.

93

Just remember—one little raindrop
Started the Johnstown flood . . . in Pennsylvania.
When you're lying on a park bench
Eating grass 'cause you've no dough,
Your luck will change mañana—
You may be six feet under, helping it grow . . .
So just remember when you're lower than low—
There's always one step further down you can go!

> (*The melody is a cheerful, childish jingle—typically Shirley Temple in character—which provides a wild contrast to the deadly message of the lyrics.* HOPE *and* LOU *caper about a bit, dancing in the Temple-Robinson manner, complete with patriotic taps and off-to-Buffalos, then resume singing*)

LOU

Don't be afraid of a little rumble . . .
What's that, for goodness' sake?
Just remember—one little rumble
Started the Frisco quake . . .

HOPE

In Pennsylvania?

BOTH

When you're lying on a park bench
Eating grass 'cause you've no dough . . .

LOU

Your luck will change mañana—

HOPE

You may be six feet under, helping it grow . . .

94

LOU

So just remember when you're lower than low—

BOTH

There's always one step further down you can go!
(*As they finish, they are exhilarated momentarily by the effort they've put out. Then they bow and curtsy to each other, don their sandwich signs again, and resume handing out blotters, walking in opposite directions*)

LOU Take one, sir? Come to Madame Barrymore's— Queen of Terpsichore. Tap-tap-tap your way to movie fame . . .
(LOU *exits*)

HOPE Have you got a Shirley Temple in your home? Send her to Madame Barrymore's . . . (*A girl passes in one direction, as several men walk by in another. One of the men is* RUDOLF, *who suddenly recognizes her*) Thank you, lady! Baby takes a bow!

RUDOLF (*Grabbing her sign and turning her to him*) Hope!

HOPE (*Turning away from him*) Go away!

RUDOLF (*Following her*) Hope . . .

HOPE (*Turns on him*) This is an excellent job and I don't want to lose it! (*Turning to a passer-by, in a sweet Shirley Temple voice*) Have you got a Shirley Temple in your home?

95

RUDOLF   Hope, why didn't you get in touch with me?

HOPE   Beat it! You . . . nephew! You . . . you—vice-president!

RUDOLF   (*Forcing her to face him*)   You've got to listen to me . . .

HOPE   (*In full fury*)   All right! Now you can tell your Uncle Lionel you found me . . . and got me fired . . . and you can get yourself another big, fat promotion! (*A couple are passing by.* HOPE *steps into their path with all her rage and vents it on them*) HAVE YOU GOT A SHIRLEY TEMPLE IN YOUR HOME!
   (*The couple freeze in terror for a moment, then stumble off, looking back at her*)

RUDOLF   I—I don't want a promotion—I want *you*! And the only thing I'm going to tell Uncle Lionel is that he can't do things like this . . .

HOPE   (*Tired now*)   Oh, Rudolf, what's the use? You'd only get yourself fired . . .

RUDOLF   (*Intensely*)   I'll get you a better job! I'll get you back on the set—with me! I'll disguise you! I'm not going to let you out of my sight again!
   (*He gets inside the sandwich sign with her*)

HOPE   Oh, look, Rudolf, I'm doing very well—on my own!

RUDOLF   (*Embracing her*)   I love you!

HOPE This job could lead to almost *anything!* All kinds of important people come down this street . . .

RUDOLF I love you!
(*She hears him this time, looks over her shoulder at him, melts and turns to him—they kiss. At this moment a dowdy, imposing harridan enters*)

WOMAN (*Stops, pointing at* HOPE) You!

HOPE (*Breaking the embrace*) Madame Barrymore!

WOMAN Soliciting on the job! The cops are gonna hear about this!
(*Screeching, she rushes out*)

HOPE *and* RUDOLF (HOPE *gives a hopeless shrug, as she and* RUDOLF *dance off together, inside the sign. Singing*)
There's always one step further down . . .
There's always one step further down . . .
There's always one step further down . . .
You can go!

Blackout

Scene Four

L.Z. GOVERNOR'S *office. The office and its furnishings suggest the 1930's motif—there is an excess of chrome trimming and blue plush. On one side is a desk and chair. On the desk are a telephone and an Oscar, and near the desk stands an easel with an elaborate poster on it, announcing:* "F.F.F. STUDIOS *present* THE FIDDLER AND THE FIGHTER." *On the other side of the room are a large plush couch, and a chair near it.* L.Z. *is lying on the couch, and* DR. TRAURIG *sits near him, in the chair, in the process of a word-association test.*

TRAURIG Happiness.

L.Z. (*Ecstatically*) Lila!

TRAURIG George Washington.

L.Z. Lila. (*The telephone rings*) Lila. (L.Z. *jumps up, going to his desk. Into the phone*) Yes, my little Heifetz? What? The New York office? (*Angry*) Put 'em on! What? The picture's practically finished! So what if it took eighty-two days? It's my idiot nephew's fault! The girl's great! Don't bother me. Goodbye. (*He puts down the phone*) All right . . . (*He goes back to the couch*)

TRAURIG So you're happy.

L.Z. (*Sitting on the couch*) I'm happy! I'm in love!

TRAURIG And you brought me six thousand miles and kept me here *two months* . . . and that is all I can get out of you? We have cured only one symptom . . . not your basic trouble.

L.Z. I'm in love—I'm happy! If I could only get some sleep . . .

TRAURIG Lie down. (L.Z. *lies down*) Let us go back again to the *beginning* . . .

L.Z. (*Sings, in a turgidly dramatic operatic manner, "The Dangerous Age"*)

> When young I had no time for fun—
> At fourteen I worked for a furrier.
> Before I was young my youth was done—
> I was a hurrier and worrier.
> (*Getting up, pacing*)
> Then I bought a concession at Coney;
> A good investment it proved—
> Nickelodeon machines they called them—
> You looked in at pictures that moved.
> And then I went to the West Coast—
> My empire started to grow.
> I founded the F.F.F. Studios,
> And became the giant, you know!
> But all the time, like at the furrier—
> A worrier and a hurrier!
> (*Speaking*)
> Work . . . work . . . work . . . work . . . work!

99

(*Singing*)
I feel I've been cheated of my youth—
And that's—*E pluribus unum*—the truth!
But now I'm forgetting the drudgery of my past . . .
I've found someone who makes me feel young at
     last . . .
(*Suddenly he breaks into a corny pop tune, in the
style of the Charleston era, which he performs in
a frantic, somewhat Eddie Cantor manner*)
Every night I dream of her, dream of her, dream of
     her—
Every night I dream of her
'Cause I'm at the dangerous age—Yip! Yip! Yip!

Feeling like a boy again,
Playing with a toy again,
Bubbling up with joy again,
'Cause I'm at the dangerous age . . .
I just don't feel like working any more—
Want to kick off my shoes and dance barefoot on the
     shore,
For . . .

Every night I dream of her, dream of her, dream of
     her—
Scheme and scheme and dream of her . . .
'Cause I'm at the dangerous age—
And I love it—
I'm at the dangerous age—
Can't help it—
I'm at the dangerous age!
(L.Z. *lies back down on the couch as the song
finishes*)

TRAURIG And yet you wake up every night in a cold sweat . . . because of your souped-up sexual drives . . .

L.Z. (*Sits up*) Sex again! Stop talking dirty . . . you dirty, dirty man! (*Suddenly upset*) It's the *other* girl I want to get out of my dreams—

TRAURIG (*Leaning forward*) What other girl?

L.Z. (*On his feet now*) The *wrong* girl—the one I fired! She turns up every place!

TRAURIG (*Excited*) Aha! We're getting somewhere at last! You never mentioned her before! Now tell me the *whole* dream . . .

L.Z. (*Pacing*) It's not a dream—it's a nightmare! The dreams start out as I told you . . . but something always happens . . . and I suddenly find myself in the middle of one of my own musical pictures. But they won't let it come out the way I want it to! I find myself in a forest . . . surrounded by beautiful girls . . . I'm playing a fiddle! But things keep going wrong!
 (*Even as* L.Z. *describes his nightmare, his office dissolves into the setting of his dream: desk, walls, chairs, couch, and* DR. TRAURIG *are spirited out of sight . . . and in their place a gigantic, shimmering golden tree appears. Golden nymphs fly to surround* L.Z., *as if by magic, and suddenly his business suit becomes a suit of Don Juan tights, and in his hands are a violin and bow . . . which he plays like a virtuoso, throughout his dream.*

In the ballet that follows, L.Z. is the ecstatic ob-
server of golden nymphs and satyrs at play among
a forest of statuesque trees—that is, beautiful showgirls whose peacock-tail gowns suggest golden
foliage. Among the nymphs and satyrs, L.Z. dis-
covers GLORIA, glittering in dewy jewels from head
to toe . . . and, inspired by the caprices of the
dancers, L.Z. pursues her . . . aided and abetted by
a satanic gold master of the revels, and a lithe
golden Cupid. The general effect strongly suggests
the look of the grand foyer of a neighborhood
Loew's movie palace.

There is only one problem in this pursuit of
L.Z.'s heart's desire—and that is HOPE SPRINGFIELD.
Each time L.Z. is about to attain the unattainable,
HOPE somehow springs eternally in GLORIA's place
—first as a manicurist, then as an usherette, later
as a waitress. Impatiently, L.Z. dismisses her from
his dream, pantomiming "Out! Out!" The satyrs
carry her off time and time again, but she re-appears
on schedule, a true nightmare figure.

At last, assisted into silken gold robe and pajamas
and crowned with golden laurel, L.Z. approaches
an enormous golden bed—as nymphs and satyrs
form the canopies. He puts his violin aside and pre-
pares to join at last what he believes to be GLORIA
—when, pulling aside the covers, he finds, not
GLORIA, not even HOPE, but DR. TRAURIG, shaking
his finger reprovingly at L.Z., as nymphs, satyrs and
the bed itself collapse in garish pandemonium, with
L.Z. screaming in anguish and frustration as the
lights fade)

Scene Five

On the set, with light bridge and scenery pieces still in view on the sound stage, a rehearsal is going on for the last scene of the picture The Fiddler and the Fighter. *It is a wedding reception, and extras are standing in their places, all facing an offstage camera. The extras, as wedding guests, are arranged in two separate groups—the group at stage right are all society types, dressed in morning coats, striped trousers, gray top hats, spats and gloves; they are with their ladies, who are in white formal gowns. The other group, at left, are working-class types, all dressed shabbily, with grimy faces, tattered coats and battered hats. Between the two groups stands* BYRON (*or Kid*), *the groom, in formal wedding attire.* RUDOLF *is seated in the canvas director's chair, holding the shooting script.*

RUDOLF   All right, everybody . . . (*He blows his whistle*) Let's rehearse the wedding scene. Remember, the wedding cake will be—right here. (*He goes to indicate an area at center stage, then back to his chair, calling offstage*) Miss Tremaine! On the set, please! (*As* GLORIA *enters hurriedly, wearing a bridal gown and veils and carrying a bouquet*) You're late . . . again.

GLORIA   You're always rushing me!
　　(*She goes to her place beside* BYRON)

RUDOLF   All right—action!

BYRON (*Singing*)
> I'm with you—
> I won't change partners 'cause . . .
>
> My heart is like a violin—
> The tune comes out when you come in . . .
>> (*He and* GLORIA *exchange a look—it's* their *song
>> now, and he's finally gotten it into the picture*)

CHORUS (*Switching to "The Fiddler and the Fighter"*)
> Whether you're a fiddler or a fighter—

BYRON
> You're first and foremost an American!

CHORUS
> A great big battleship or cruiser

BYRON
> Can sail no better than a ferry can!

CHORUS
> So grab your fiddle . . .

BYRON
> Put on your gloves . . .
> And sing along with me—

ALL
> Whether you're a fiddler or a fighter—

BYRON (*Going down on one knee, Jolson style*)
> That's a Broadway melody!

RUDOLF (*Blowing his whistle*) All right . . . let's run
the lines now. All right, Miss Tremaine.

GLORIA (*As Griselda*) "We're very proud that you're all here . . . our Park Avenue admirers . . . and our old friends from the wuppah . . ."

BYRON (*As Kid*) "Yeah, and all my buddies from . . ."

RUDOLF (*Interrupting, blows his whistle again. He rises, showing* GLORIA *the script*) Miss Tremaine . . . you said "wuppah." You see, it isn't "wuppah" . . . it's "W.P.A." Those are initials which stand for the Works Projects Administration.

GLORIA (*As if understanding for the first time*) Oh . . . initials! Oh!

RUDOLF (*Going back to his chair*) Right! Again, please . . .

GLORIA "We're very proud that you're all here . . . (*Turns to the shabby group*) our Park Avenue admirers . . . and our—" (RUDOLF *blows his whistle; she stops*) What's wrong?

RUDOLF (*Again rises and goes to* GLORIA. BYRON *moves away a bit, looking bored*) Well, you turned to the wrong group . . . you see, on your *right* are the "Park Avenue admirers" and on your *left* are your "old friends from the wuppah"—uh—the W.P.A.! (*Shaking his head, he goes back to his chair*) Once more, please!
(RUDOLF *sits*)

GLORIA "You are very proud that we're all here . . ."
(RUDOLF *blows his whistle; she stops*)

RUDOLF Wrong line, Miss Tremaine.

105

GLORIA (*Heatedly*) No wonder I can't remember! You get me so nervous . . . blowing that damned whistle! I need a few minutes of peace and quiet in my dressing room!
> (*She turns abruptly and goes off, giving* BYRON *a quick look.* BYRON, *a little wearily, ambles off after her, whistling a few bars of "Close Harmony"*)

RUDOLF (*To the company*) Take five! (*The extras begin to drift offstage, and* RUDOLF *moves to where a male extra dressed in morning coat, striped trousers, spats, gloves and top hat, with a black Chaplinesque moustache, has moved away from the group, to sit in a chair. Behind his hand, to the male extra*) So far, so good.

HOPE (*For it is indeed she—in disguise*) Yeah, a couple of the girls in the cast want my phone number!
> (*She quickly turns away and huddles down into the chair as* L.Z. *and* DR. TRAURIG *enter, arguing.* RUDOLF *moves to his director's chair, pretending to study the script*)

TRAURIG (*As they enter*) Mr. Governor . . . you asked my opinion!

L.Z. And I tell you, she's my greatest discovery!

TRAURIG She'll make a monkey out of you . . . you, with your obsessive sex drive . . .

L.Z. Sex again! You *dirty* man! You *dirty, dirty* man!

TRAURIG (*Exploding at last*) I am sick of your accusations. I am *not* a dirty man. It is *you* who are dirty!

L.Z. Me . . . dirty? No! No . . . *you* are dirty!

TRAURIG (*Wagging his finger furiously*) I am not the *dirty* one! *You* . . . It is *you* who are *dirty* . . .

L.Z. (*Boiling*) Me? *Me*? Dirty? You—*You* are dirty!!

TRAURIG (*Shouting*) I am *not* dirty!

L.Z. (*Turning away*) I don't need a dirty man like you . . . (*Turns back to* TRAURIG) You're *fired!* Go back where you came from . . . you foreigner!

TRAURIG (*Quietly, intensely, holding his ground*) I am staying here! I have already more patients than I can handle! Some of the town's biggest biggies! (*Now, with full Patrick Henry nobility*) America is still a nation of pioneers—but, thank God, they are sick *pioneers!*
 (*He stomps out.* L.Z. *watches* TRAURIG *for a moment, then turns and speaks to* RUDOLF)

L.Z. Huh. And that nut is trying to tell me how to make pictures. The girl's great . . . Right, Rudolf? (RUDOLF *remains absorbed in his script, making no reply*) Right, Rudolf?

RUDOLF (*Taking a deep breath, looks up*) No. (L.Z. *can't quite believe what he has heard*) The girl's terrible! And . . . and the picture's terrible too! It's only an hour and a half long . . . but you sit there . . . it seems like yearly a near!

L.Z. (*Confused*) What did you say?

RUDOLF (*Shouting*) I don't know! (*Catches his breath*) You want to preview this film tonight? Well, you better come dressed as an old lady . . . or they're going to tear you to pieces!

L.Z. (*Firmly*) Rudolf, shoot the last scene and finish the picture!

(*He turns and starts to walk off*)

RUDOLF (*Shouts*) Wait! (*Advancing to* L.Z.) I didn't burn the film! I took it home.

L.Z. What film?

RUDOLF (*Building in intensity*) The Fiddler and the Fighter . . . starring Hope Springfield! (*At this,* HOPE, *who has been hiding her face, turns to listen*) Did you ever take the trouble to look at the picture?

L.Z. (*Dismissing him, turns away*) I didn't hear a word you said . . . I didn't hear it!

RUDOLF Well, *I've* seen it! And . . . and I'll tell you something . . . She's different . . . remarkable! Like . . . like a wonderful sunset in the morning! I mean—something you've never seen before! An original! *A star!* And that's the picture you ought to preview tonight!

L.Z. (*Intoning slowly, like one hypnotized*) Tonight you will preview *this* picture! And, remember, keep Lila on the set after the shooting . . . there's going to be a surprise! (*He exits.* RUDOLF *stands shaking his head. He turns to look at* HOPE, *who rises, beaming proudly at him. He comes to her and they embrace passionately. This would be a touching moment, except for the fact that to the naked eye,* RUDOLF *is kissing an odd little man with a moustache.* L.Z. *re-enters and sees this strange sight. Without changing his expression*) I didn't see a thing . . . I didn't see it!

(*He exits hastily.* HOPE *and* RUDOLF *turn and break*

their embrace . . . both laughing. She removes her
moustache)

HOPE   Rudolf . . . this is the end of your career!

RUDOLF   It's the beginning of my life . . .

HOPE   *(Tenderly)*   Mine, too . . .
      (Sings "Fade In—Fade Out")
      Close up—unhappy girl . . .
      Enter boy—Fade out!
      Fade in—a happy girl . . .
      She has her boy—Fade out!
      My life now has that moment sublime—
      I could sell it to the movies any time . . .

      My life story
      Was not a story
      You'd ever see on the silver screen.
      Everything a plot has got was missing . . .
      No suspense, no kissing,
      No laughs, no color—
      It went from dull to duller.
      Then came someone—
      Some special someone—
      Who changed my life as described above.
      Now my story's full of thrills, chills, action—
      It's a main attraction . . .
      I feel my pulse beat quickening—
      I know the plot is thickening—
      Fade out—Fade in . . .
      I've fallen in love!

RUDOLF
      Now my story's full of thrills, chills, action—

You're my main attraction . . .
I feel my pulse beat quickening—
I know the plot is thickening—
Fade out—Fade in . . .
I've fallen in . . .

BOTH

Fade out—Fade in . . .
I've fallen in love!
(*She ends up in his arms.* VESPERS *enters, calling
to* RUDOLF)

VESPERS   All right, Rudolf, ready for the wedding scene!

RUDOLF (*Still holding* HOPE's *hands, he calls*) Places!
(*To* HOPE) Meet me tonight in front of Grauman's
Chinese at ten-thirty . . .

VESPERS (*Offstage*) Mr. Prong! Miss Tremaine! On the
set, please! Places, everyone!
(*Two stagehands wheel in a large wedding cake,
placing it near the center, as* BYRON *enters.* HOPE
has moved away from RUDOLF, *straightening her
costume and re-applying her moustache.* GLORIA
enters and eyes HOPE *suspiciously.* HOPE *gives her
a quick wink as she passes and, twirling her moustache, she strolls jauntily out*)

RUDOLF   Miss Tremaine, after we finish shooting, don't
go back to your dressing room . . .

GLORIA   Why not?

RUDOLF   Mr. Governor is planning something . . . (*He
turns and goes off, calling*) Raise that camera!

GLORIA (*Annoyed*) Him and his plans! I'm so bored with them! (*She turns to* BYRON—*they are alone on stage now, near the cake*) Oh, Byron—(*Gleefully*) I can't wait till it's over! Then I can be with you all the time!

BYRON (*Quietly, cautious*) You kidding? What about L.Z.? Anyway . . . I've got to get down to the desert— rebuild my face.
    (BYRON *has his top hat in his hands in front of him. Appraisingly, he smiles into it; then, as he turns around, still looking into it, we see that there is a mirror inside the hat*)

GLORIA (*Hugging him*) That's wonderful, lover boy— I'll go with you!

BYRON (*Breaking away from her, looking around nervously, trying to whisper*) Shh! Watch it! L.Z.'s got spies all over the joint . . .

GLORIA (*Loudly*) Oh, I don't need L.Z. any more—I'm a star! He's a stupid, boring, dirty old man!
    (*And through the top of the wedding cake pops the head of* L.Z., *covered with frosting. He is wild-eyed and gesturing furiously*)

L.Z. (*Roaring*) *Surprise!* (GLORIA *and* BYRON *spring apart, backing away from the cake*) You dirty rat! You tramp! Out! Out! Out!

(*The lights fade quickly*)

Scene Six

In front of Grauman's Chinese Theatre. We see the pagoda-like front of the famed building, and in the distance, the tops of palm trees. There are posters flanking the ornate double doors leading into the theatre, and on the column-supported marquee in front of the theatre is a large banner announcing the "Major Studio Preview" taking place inside.

RUDOLF, in black tie, comes out through the double doors; he is excited as he looks around and checks his watch. A moment later, ROSCOE comes running out, pad and pencil in hand.

ROSCOE *(Yelling to RUDOLF as he exits)*   Great!

> *(RUDOLF hurries back to the theatre entrance and opens one of the doors to look and listen. HOPE enters, in street clothes, carrying a white corsage. RUDOLF turns and sees her)*

RUDOLF *(Running to her)*   Hope!

HOPE   I bought myself a corsage for you to give me. *(He takes it from her . . . and, with a small bow, presents her with it)* Thank you!

RUDOLF *(As they embrace)*   The preview isn't quite over. Something seems to be happening in there . . .

HOPE *(Let down)*   You mean . . . she's good?

RUDOLF   Never mind that . . . After this is over, let's go back to my place.

HOPE   Sure . . .

RUDOLF   I'll get some beer and sandwiches . . .

HOPE   Wonderful.

RUDOLF   And then . . .

HOPE   And then?

RUDOLF   *Monkey Business* . . . (*She looks at him startled*) with the Marx Brothers.

HOPE (*Laughing*)   Oh, Rudolf!
   (*They embrace*)

RUDOLF   And then there's something I want to tell you about *your* picture . . .

HOPE   You can burn that now, Rudolf. You've got the original in glorious technicolor . . .
   (L.Z. *bursts through the doors, rushing out of the theatre, followed by* RALPH *and the other nephews*)

L.Z.   Where is she? Where is she?
   (*He sees* HOPE *and starts toward her*)

HOPE (*Turning to him*)   You can't kick me out of here . . . this is a public street!

L.Z. (*Kneeling beside her*) Let me kiss the hem of your skirt (HOPE *is stunned, glances to* RUDOLF) Forgive a blind, stupid old man . . .

HOPE (*Thoroughly taken aback*) Rudolf . . . what's he doing?

L.Z. (*Rising*) You are sensational. You are unusual—different! Like . . . like a beautiful sunset in the morning! I didn't see the light . . . (*To his nephews*) I was an idiot, wasn't I?

NEPHEWS Yes, you were an idiot . . .

RALPH A stupid old man!

L.Z. (*Glares a moment at* RALPH *then turns back to* HOPE) Lila Tremaine . . . You are an original—a *star!*

HOPE But I'm not Lila Tremaine . . . Gloria Currie is!

L.Z. Never heard of her! I picked *you,* Number Five! Deep down in my deepest gut, I must have meant you all the time! Tonight . . . in there . . . on that screen . . . it was *you!*

HOPE What!

L.Z. My wonderful nephew, Rudolf! The film he previewed tonight was *The Fiddler and the Fighter* with *you* in it. The picture Ralphie made! Rudolf . . . Ralph . . . (RUDOLF *and* RALPH *go to him; he puts his arms*

*around their shoulders and looks proudly from one to
the other)* Kiss me!

*(Reluctantly, they kiss him on his cheek as he
beams unashamedly.* HOPE *stands to one side, dazed
and happy, until a crowd of fans come rushing out
of the theatre. They catch sight of* HOPE *and run
to her. She shrinks back, terrified)*

FANS There she is! There she is!
*(Shouting "It's Lila Tremaine!" "There she is!"
etc. They surround her. One fan grabs her sleeve,
which comes off. Inspired, several more fans reach
for similar souvenirs—and in a few seconds they
leave her standing there in nothing but shoes, hat,
and underwear)*

HOPE *(Grinning delightedly, and coyly attempting to cover
herself with her hands)* Oh, thank you! Thank you!

Blackout

Scene Seven

*In front of Grauman's Chinese Theatre—five years later.
A spotlight picks out* DORA DAILEY, *standing at her microphone.*

DORA   Oh, members of the radio audience . . . what a
thrilling occasion this is! We are broadcasting from the
front of Grauman's Chinese Theatre—one of the great
American shrines, second only to the Lincoln Memorial!
Everyone who is anyone is here tonight . . . (*The lights
come up. It is Grauman's Chinese Theatre—but five
years later—and now the entire marquee is alight with
letters:* "L-I-L-A T-R-E-M-A-I-N-E." *Crowds of fans are
cheering and jostling behind the ropes where ushers
stand guard. From inside the theatre, through the double
doors, come a parade of glamorous stars in glamorous
1930's gowns, on the arms of the nephews. The crowd
goes wild with shouts and applause as they enter—the
stars pose, blow kisses, wave and smile and sign autographs. At last* L.Z. *and* RUDOLF *enter, and stand on both
sides of the doors . . . expectantly*) Tonight . . . Lila
Tremaine . . . who gave us those great performances in
Sing, Boy, Sing—Smile, Girl, Smile—and Dance,
Barn, Dance . . . will join the immortals in the cement
in front of Grauman's Chinese Theatre.
    (*There is a fanfare as an usher comes through the
doors, carrying a wooden frame, in which is the
cement square. It is* BYRON PRONG, *now reduced to*

the job of usher. He places the square at center and puts a small pillow near it. BYRON *looks around— wanting to be remembered—and starts singing desperately)*

BYRON

My heart is like a violin . . .

L.Z. *(In a flash)* Out! Out!!
(Two fellow ushers leap forward and forcibly remove BYRON, *who keeps singing till he is dragged off)*

DORA *(Covering up)* A slight interruption . . . That, ladies and gentlemen, was a voice from yesteryear . . . And here she is now . . . Miss Lila Tremaine!
(The crowd cheer and applaud wildly as HOPE *enters through the double doors. She wears a glittering tiara . . . and yards and yards of fur wrapped around her. She bows to her fans and then moves grandly toward the microphone. At the microphone, she pauses for a moment, then silences the cheering with a simple gesture. There is instant silence, as if she switched off a radio)*

HOPE *(Into the microphone—as Janet Gaynor did it in* A Star Is Born) This is . . . Mrs. Rudolf Governor.

DORA *(Sighs ecstatically)* Ohhhhh!
*(*HOPE *throws her a glance, which silences* DORA, *then glides back to* RUDOLF, *at center. It is a hushed moment.* RUDOLF *takes off her fur wrap and holds*

it. *The crowd gasps audibly at the sight of her gown, and the glamorous greatness encased therein*)

HOPE (*Reacting regally to the sound; after all, it is her due*) I know . . . I know.
(*For a moment she takes a star pose—reminiscent of Jean Harlow's in* Hell's Angels)

DORA (*Tingling with expectation*) And now . . . at this very moment . . . she is about to leave in the cement . . . the imprint of her famous . . . smile!
(*The fans cheer again as* HOPE *kneels on the pillow and flashes—like a prop—her famous smile. Then she lowers her face into the cement. There is wild cheering. It stops. For a moment of silence she is motionless . . . then we see that* HOPE *is struggling to get up. Hands on the sides of the frame, face hidden in the cement, she tugs and pushes, and we hear her stifled mumbles. The crowd freezes . . .* L.Z. *and* RUDOLF *frantically rush to her, grab her arms, and start tugging. As they keep pulling desperately, to no avail, the music swells . . . And the curtain falls*)